Stages of Literacy Development

Stages of Literacy Development

Integrating Reading and Writing

Edited by Lin Carver

ROWMAN & LITTLEFIELD
Lanham • Boulder • New York • London

Published by Rowman & Littlefield
An imprint of The Rowman & Littlefield Publishing Group, Inc.
4501 Forbes Boulevard, Suite 200, Lanham, Maryland 20706
www.rowman.com

86-90 Paul Street, London EC2A 4NE

Copyright © 2023 by Lin Carver

All rights reserved. No part of this book may be reproduced in any form or by any electronic or mechanical means, including information storage and retrieval systems, without written permission from the publisher, except by a reviewer who may quote passages in a review.

British Library Cataloguing in Publication Information Available

Library of Congress Cataloging-in-Publication Data

Names: Carver, Lin, 1955- editor.
  Title: Stages of literacy development : integrating reading and writing / edited by Lin Carver.
  Description: Lanham, Maryland : Rowman & Littlefield, 2023. | Includes bibliographical references and index. | Summary: "The book focuses on integrating reading and writing instruction at each stage of literacy development"-- Provided by publisher.
  Identifiers: LCCN 2022046341 (print) | LCCN 2022046342 (ebook) | ISBN 9781475870022 (cloth) | ISBN 9781475870039 (paperback) | ISBN 9781475870046 (ebook)
  Subjects: LCSH: Reading--United States. | Composition (Language arts)--United States. | Language arts--Correlation with content subjects.
  Classification: LCC LB1050 .S69 2023 (print) | LCC LB1050 (ebook) | DDC 372.4--dc23/eng/20221123
  LC record available at https://lccn.loc.gov/2022046341
  LC ebook record available at https://lccn.loc.gov/2022046342

This book is dedicated to friends and colleagues who are making a difference daily in the lives of learners of all ages by guiding them through the stages of literacy development, integrating opportunities and strategies to enhance reading and writing development.

Contents

Preface	xix
Chapter 1: Stages of Literacy Development *Lin Carver*	1
Anticipation Guide	2
What Is Literacy?	2
Changing Literacy Skills	3
Methods of Literacy Instruction	4
Phonics versus Whole Language	4
Balanced versus Structured Literacy	4
Simple View versus Active View of Reading	5
Reading and Writing as Reciprocal Processes	6
Reading and Writing Ropes	7
Stages of Reading and Writing Development	10
Anticipation Guide Revisited	12
Conclusion	12
Stop and Think	13
References	13
Chapter 2: Emergent Stage *Gretchen Rudolph-Fladd and Lin Carver*	17
Anticipation Guide	17

Characteristics of Emergent Readers	18
Role of Oral Language	19
Concept of Word	19
Phonological Awareness	20
Rhyming	20
Syllables	21
Phonemic Awareness	22
Onset-Rime	22
Developing Concepts of Print	23
Environmental Print	24
Function of Letters	24
Characteristics of Text for Emergent Readers	24
Characteristics of Emergent Writers	25
Instructional Methods for Emergent Readers	25
Using Texts with Emergent Readers	26
Wordless Books	27
Picture Walk	27
Point around the Picture	28
Predictable Pattern Books	28
Leader and Chorus Choral Reading	28
Predictable Charts	29
Nursery Rhymes	29
Rhyming	30
Rhyme Time	30
Rhyming Books	31
Describing Characters	31
Share the Pen	31
ABC Books	31

Concepts of Print	32
Collaborative Writing	32
Picture Books	33
Draw a Prediction	33
T Chart Lists	34
Anticipation Guide Revisited	34
Conclusion	35
Stop and Think	35
References	36
Chapter 3: Beginning Stage	**41**
Cheri Gallman and Lin Carver	
Anticipation Guide	42
Characteristics of Beginning Readers	42
Concept of Word	43
Sight Words and High-Frequency Words	43
Phonics Skills	44
Language and Vocabulary Development	45
Reading Connected Text	46
Characteristics of Texts for Beginning Readers	47
Characteristics of Beginning Writers	48
Instructional Methods	48
Gradual Release	49
Using Texts with Beginning Readers	49
Teacher Created	49
Fill-in-the-Blank Message	50
Elkonin Boxes	50
Word Ladders	50
Interactive Writing	51

Decodable Texts	52
Repeated Readings	52
Echo Reading	53
Twister Spell and Read	53
Leveled Readers	53
Leader and Chorus Choral Reading	54
Class Book	54
Nonfiction-Informational Text	54
KWL	55
Cross-Grade Reading Buddies	55
Sketch to Stretch	55
Beginning Reader Fiction Series	55
Think Aloud	56
Stop and Jot	56
Anticipation Guide Revisited	57
Conclusion	57
Stop and Think	57
References	58
Chapter 4: Transitional Stage	**63**
Janet Deck	
Anticipation Guide	63
Characteristics of the Transitional Stage	64
Transitional Readers	64
Diphthongs	64
Sight Words	65
Comprehension	65
Characteristics of Transitional Text	66
Transitional Writers	66

Fairy Tales	67
Story Map	68
Closed Compare/Contrast Graphic Organizer	68
Easy Chapter Books	68
SWBS	69
SWBST	69
SWBSF	69
POV Response	70
Fantasy	70
Buddy Reading	71
Field Notes with Pictures	72
Mystery	72
Text Talk	73
First-Person Journals	73
Self-Help	73
Think-Pair-Share	74
SEL Writing Prompt	75
Anticipation Guide Revisited	75
Conclusion	76
Stop and Think	76
References	76
Chapter 5: Intermediate Stage *Janet Deck*	79
Anticipation Guide	80
Characteristics of Intermediate Readers	80
Decoding Multisyllabic Words	81
Inflectional Suffixes	81
Primary and Secondary Sources	81

Figurative Language	82
Characteristics of Texts for Intermediate Readers	83
Syntax	83
Academic Language	84
Structural Analysis	84
Motivation	85
Characteristics of Intermediate Writers	85
Paraphrasing and Note-Taking	85
Writing Conventions	86
Nonfiction-Informational Texts	86
Probable Passage	87
Text Reformulation	88
Tall Tales	89
Prediction Relay	89
T Chart Graphic Organizer	89
Write a Tall Tale	90
Myths	90
Graphic Organizer for Note-Taking	91
Research Writing	91
Online Post	91
Comics	92
Matching Texts with Comics	92
It Says–I Say–and So	92
Comic Strip Creator	93
Advertisements/Social Media	94
Loaded Words	94
Create an Advertisement	94
Anticipation Guide Revisited	94

Conclusion	95
Stop and Think	95
References	95
Chapter 6: Proficient Stage	**99**
Cheri Gallman and Lin Carver	
Anticipation Guide	100
Middle School: A Time of Change	100
Physical Changes	101
Social Changes	101
Emotional Changes	101
Cognitive Changes	102
The Adolescent Brain	102
Impact of Brain Development on Instruction	103
Characteristics of Proficient Readers	103
More Complex Texts	104
Strategies for Decoding Multisyllabic Words	104
Academic Language	105
Disciplinary Literacy	107
History	108
Science	108
Mathematics	109
Reading and Evaluating Online Resources	109
Characteristics of Struggling Middle School Readers	110
Juicy Sentences	110
Characteristics of Texts for Proficient Readers	111
Types of Writing for Middle School	111
Academic Writing	112
Digital Writing	112

Biographies and Autobiographies	112
Fishbowl Discussion	112
Venn Diagram	113
Historical Fiction	113
Dump and Clump	114
Narrative Pyramid	114
Dystopia	115
Personal Word List	115
Concept Cubes	115
3–2–1	116
Scientific Articles	116
Adjusting Lexile Level	116
Academic Language	117
Vocabulary Knowledge Scale	117
Close Read	118
ABC Graphic Organizer	119
Graphic Novels	119
Semantic Feature Map	120
Padlet	120
Anticipation Guide Revisited	120
Conclusion	121
Stop and Think	121
References	121
Chapter 7: Multiple Views	**127**
Lisa Ciganek	
Anticipation Guide	128
High School Readers and Writers	128
What Is a Complex Text?	129

Multiple View Skill Development	131
Increased Self-Efficacy	131
Increased Relevance	131
Expanded Skills	132
Mastering Structural Analysis	132
Vocabulary Instruction	133
New Skills	133
Additional Figurative Language	134
Archetypes	134
Developing Arguments	135
Fallacies in Arguments	136
Written Structure and Syntax Skills	136
Active versus Passive Voice	136
Grammatical Structures	137
Genre Reading and Writing Strategies	137
Drama	138
Character Double-Entry Journal	138
Character Résumé	139
Speeches	140
Student-Constructed Concept Map	140
RAFT	141
Text Structure	142
Blogs	142
Text Scavenger Hunt	143
Argumentative Text	143
Annotation	143
Backwards Outlining	145
Poetry	145

Questioning the Author	146
Original Poems	147
Anticipation Guide Revisited	147
Conclusion	147
Stop and Think	148
References	148
Chapter 8: Readers with Learning Disabilities and Learning Differences *Marian Moore-Taylor and Lin Carver*	151
Anticipation Guide	152
Speech Acquisition versus Reading Development	152
High School versus College and Career Reading Levels	153
What Is a Learning Disability?	153
Specific Learning Disabilities	155
Non-Reading-Related Learning Disabilities	155
Dyscalculia	155
Dysgraphia	156
Nonverbal Learning Disabilities	157
Attention-Deficit/Hyperactivity Disorder (ADHD)	157
Dyspraxia	158
Executive Dysfunction	158
Reading Difficulty vs. Reading Disorder: What's the Difference?	159
Types of Reading Disorders	159
Dyslexia	159
Supporting Students with Reading Difficulties and Disabilities	160
Accommodations	161
Modifications	161
Comprehension Difficulties	161

Basic Processing Weaknesses	162
Long-Term Memory Difficulties	162
Short-Term or Working Memory Difficulties	163
Phonological Processing Difficulties	163
Difficulties in the Sound-Symbol Relationship	163
Digital Resources	164
Note-Taking	164
Speech-to-Text	164
Text-to-Speech	164
Abbreviation Expanders	165
Alternative Keyboards	165
Audiobooks and Publications	165
Electronic Math Worksheets	165
Graphic Organizers and Outlining	165
Optical Character Recognition	166
Personal FM Listening Systems	166
Proofreading Programs	166
Talking Calculators	166
Talking Spell Checkers and Electronic Dictionaries	166
Word Prediction Programs	167
Anticipation Guide Revisited	167
Conclusion	167
Stop and Think	167
References	168
Index	173
About the Editor and Contributors	177

Preface

Progress in literacy development across the United States has not occurred at the level we would like to see, and we are not making significant progress to change this trend. Recently released federal data, based on assessments made just before the pandemic lockdown in early 2020, showed flat scores for elementary students, while scores for middle schoolers were declining. The National Assessment of Educational Progress (NAEP) records the reading proficiency levels of fourth, eighth, and twelfth graders in school districts across the United States, based on a scale from 0 to 500. Scores are recorded across the Basic, Proficient, and Advanced performance levels. Reading scores have only changed minimally in the past 27 years, moving from 217 to 220 for all fourth-grade students, from 260 to 263 for all eighth-grade students, and from 292 to 287 for all twelfth-grade students. In order to address the widespread problem of low literacy, educators must first understand the stages of reading and writing development and why so many students struggle to read.

CHAPTER COMPASS

In chapter 1, the book begins by establishing the theoretical framework for differentiating instruction based on the stages of literacy development. Chapters 2 through 7 provide information about each of the stages of literacy development: Emergent, Beginning, Transitional, Intermediate, Proficient, and Multiple Views. Chapter 8 examines issues students may experience and how teachers can support those with reading disabilities or differences.

Each chapter begins with a classroom vignette to help the reader visualize that specific stage of development. This is followed by a brief anticipation guide highlighting some of the concepts covered in the chapter. In each chapter the major characteristics of each stage are presented, and five different literary genres appropriate to that stage are discussed. For each genre, reading and writing strategies are described. The chapter concludes by providing the reader an opportunity to revisit the anticipation guide and then extend and apply their skills through Stop and Think activities that relate the content to their specific educational setting.

Chapter 1

Stages of Literacy Development

Lin Carver

Brianna Williams left her office, anxious to see how the children were settling into their new school year at Southern Elementary. Data from the state assessment had come in over the summer, and the school's grade had been disappointing. Teachers had worked hard in an attempt to have students make gains, but the effects of spotty attendance, changing instructional methods, and teacher turnover over the past two years were evident.

As she approached Ralph Jones's second-grade classroom, she knew that the literacy block should be in full swing. She opened the door, pleased with what she saw. A guided reading group of six students was seated at a round table in the back of the room echo reading the folktale "The Pied Piper" from their new reading series. Spread throughout the rest of the room, students were working individually or in pairs, busily writing or editing their own folktales that they were completing to accompany this unit. She was about to leave the room when she noticed one student, Bethanne, just looking at a blank sheet of paper. "Is everything alright?" Brianna asked.

"I don't know what to write," Bethanne complained. "I have no ideas."

"What mentor texts have you read in class?" Brianna inquired. "See if you can change the problem slightly in one of those," she suggested. "Why don't you look at some of those again for ideas?"

"I guess," Bethanne responded, not sounding convinced.

"Well, at least most of the students were engaged," Brianna thought as she left the room. The second classroom she approached was Melissa Smith's third-grade class. As she opened the door, she observed that the entire class was seated in a circle enthusiastically involved in a whole-group, student-led grand conversation about the difference between spiders and insects in preparation for in informational article they were about to read. The grand conversation was entirely student led, with Mrs. Smith participating as a member of the discussion. She only intervened a couple of times to facilitate or scaffold the conversation. The talk pattern was conversational, with students taking turns by signaling with a raised thumb that they wanted to speak. It was a really interesting discussion and seemed to be increasing background knowledge about the topic in preparation for reading.

Brianna had a few minutes before lunch duty, so she decided to visit one more classroom on her way to the cafeteria. She entered Danielle Thomas's fourth-grade classroom. Students had their journals open on their desks. Many were busy writing ideas, but quite a few were looking at the clock or out of the window. Jeffrey raised his hand. "Do we have to keep writing?" he complained. "I hate writing."

Engagement certainly was not as high as in the other classrooms she had been in, Brianna thought. Thinking about the three classrooms she had visited, Brianna wondered, "What are we going to do to increase the reading and writing scores this year? How can we make a difference for our students?" She thought about what activities she had seen during the morning and what activities she should have seen that were missing. "This would make a great conversation for the first PLC meeting of the year," she thought. The topic would be: What are the best practice literacy activities that should be evident in your classroom, and how do we engage our learners in these practices?

ANTICIPATION GUIDE

Read the following four statements before reading the chapter. Decide if you agree or disagree with each statement. Then read the chapter. After reading the chapter, revisit the anticipation guide and decide if your views are the same or have changed.

1. Literacy encompasses the same skills it did 50 years ago.
2. Reading and writing are reciprocal skills.
3. Balanced literacy and structured literacy are the same thing.
4. With the increased emphasis on literacy instruction, students' mean literacy scores on national assessments are improving.

WHAT IS LITERACY?

More than fifty years ago, International Literacy Day was instituted by the United Nations Educational, Scientific, and Cultural Organization (UNESCO). At its inception in 1966, it was calculated that about 24% of young people between the ages of 15 and 24 could not read and write (Carter,

2016). Today it is calculated that less than 10% of young people in this age group cannot read and write (Carter, 2016). This decrease is wonderful; however, there haven't just been changes in the worldwide literacy rate—expectations have changed as well.

Only a generation ago being able to read and write at an eighth-grade level was sufficient for many jobs (Wagner, 2010), but the necessary literacy skills for economic success in the United States have changed. The National Adult Literacy Survey data in 1999 indicated that nearly all employees received positive economic payoffs from higher literacy proficiencies (U.S. Department of Education, 1999). Sinclair's (2017) more recent research supported these same findings on the impact of strong literacy skills on both income and employability, even though technological advances have impacted necessary job-related skills.

Changing Literacy Skills

These advanced literacy skills needed for economic success are based on learners possessing a thorough understanding of the relationship between letters and sounds, but literacy, as we know, involves so much more. In the twenty-first century, necessary literacy skills include the ability to read, write, and use technology to problem-solve, collaborate, and present multimedia information (Pilgrim & Martinez, 2013). This growth in the digital world is expanding our understanding of literacy to include digital literacy. Digital literacy involves using information and communication technologies for locating, evaluating, creating, and communicating digital information using cognitive and technical skills (Gehsmann & Templeton, 2022).

Digital literacy does not occur in a vacuum. Many of the skills for success in digital literacy are developed through exposure to and proficiency with print literacy. The data is not encouraging there. For the first time in almost fifty years, the data from the National Assessment of Educational Progress (NAEP) is reporting decreases in the reading scores for 13-year-olds across the nation (LeBlanc, 2021).

Standardized test scores do not provide a complete picture of the state of the American educational system, but this data does raise some concerns. Findings indicate that, in particular, lower-performing students today are struggling even more than lower-performing students were a decade ago. In fact, today's learners are no longer demonstrating competency in skills that students were proficient in almost a decade ago (LeBlanc, 2021). Consequently, it is even more important for students to have teachers who can guide them through the stages of literacy development so that they can become literate with both print and digital mediums.

METHODS OF LITERACY INSTRUCTION

There has been much debate about the "best" way to provide reading instruction. Debates have continued about the advantages of phonics versus whole language (Reading Horizons, 2022), balanced literacy versus structured literacy (Lorimor-Easley & Reed, 2019), and the Simple View of Reading (Farrell et al., 2019) versus the Active View of Reading (Duke & Cartwright, 2021), which are all views that have been espoused over the last 50 years. Each of these methods has helped to expand our understanding of the reading and writing processes and has identified essential components that all teachers should incorporate in their instruction. Educators have seen many of these approaches throughout their experiences as literacy instructors, coaches, and administrators.

Phonics versus Whole Language

The original reading wars were fought over whether to provide phonics instruction or whole language instruction. Phonics-based reading instruction espouses that children should be taught to read and spell words through spelling rules and phonetic relationships (sound-symbol relationships) that will help them decode unknown words in connected text. Phonics instruction attempts to break down written language into small, simple components. In contrast, the whole language approach teaches children to read by recognizing words as whole units of language. It espouses that language should not be broken down into letters and combinations of letters and then decoded. Instead, language should be presented as a complete meaning making system, with words functioning in relation to each other in context (Reading Horizons, 2022).

Balanced versus Structured Literacy

Next came the debate between balanced literacy and structured literacy. Structured literacy is explicit, systematic teaching that focuses on phonological awareness, word recognition, phonics, decoding, spelling, and syntax at the sentence and paragraph levels. Balanced literacy, on the other hand, assumes that reading and writing are developed through instruction and support in multiple environments using various teacher-led and child-controlled approaches (Fountas & Pinnell, 2018). In balanced literacy, phonics, decoding, and spelling are frequently taught in word study lessons, but the skills typically are not emphasized or taught systematically (Spear-Swearling, 2015). Students are encouraged to use word analogies, pictures, or context to identify words rather than emphasize decoding. The balanced literacy method usually included the teacher reading aloud and asking students questions (shared reading), students reading the text in homogeneous groups and discussing it with the teacher (guided reading), and students self-selecting independent reading books (Lorimar-Easley & Reed, 2019).

Simple View versus Active View of Reading

With the publication of the 2019 nation's report card showing decreasing reading proficiency scores for fourth-graders in 17 states and eighth-graders in 31 states (LeBlanc, 2021), the Simple View of Reading has received significant attention in the last few years. Currently, the one most frequently discussed difference is between the Science of Reading and the Active View of Reading. Scarborough's rope has been used to illustrate the two major components of the Science of Reading, which were originally referred to as decoding and listening comprehension (Gough & Tunmer, 1986) and later expanded to word recognition and linguistic comprehension (Hoover & Tunmer, 2020).

In addition to word-reading and language comprehension skills, readers must learn to regulate attention, choose appropriate strategies, maintain motivation, and actively engage with the text. These components have led to the revision of the Simple View of Reading to the more extensive Active View of Reading (Duke & Cartwright, 2021). Choosing strategies and texts that are at the right developmental stage and engaging readers and writers are essential for enhancing reading and writing success.

These approaches are based on a body of investigation that encompasses years of scientific research that support an understanding of the cognitive processes essential for reading proficiency. These studies have stressed the importance of intensive phonemic awareness and phonic decoding training, as well as opportunities for repeated practice in reading controlled text. Instruction and intervention in these skills lead to efficient orthographic mapping. In this approach, emphasis on whole word memorization or configuration is limited. If children memorize ten words, then they can read ten words. But if learners can master the sounds of ten letters, they can read 350 three-sound words; 4,320 four-sound words; and 21,650 five-sound words (Ordetx, 2021).

Initial sound-symbol matching during the Emergent and Beginning stages occurs along a continuum that can be divided into three stages: letters and sounds, phonic decoding, and orthographic mapping. Letter-sound knowledge provides the foundation for phonic decoding, orthographic mapping, and sight word recognition. During the phonic decoding phase, early phonological awareness skills support the development of letter-sound knowledge and are a basis for direct instruction through first grade. The advanced phonological awareness skills should continue to be practiced and assessed through third grade to ensure the establishment of a solid orthographic lexicon. Instruction in orthographic mapping allows teachers to support students who struggle to read. Orthographic mapping is the process that occurs when unfamiliar words become automatic sight words. Orthographic mapping explains how learners develop a vast, accurate sight word bank for automatic word retrieval; its lack explains why students with reading difficulties struggle to develop this skill.

As students' phonics and phonemic manipulation skills develop, these enable students to build a sight word bank or orthographic lexicon. To support this acquisition, students need sufficient practice and review in decoding and encoding, knowledge and application of orthographic concepts, and exposure to decodable text. However, just automatically identifying words is not enough. Comprehension is the ultimate goal of reading. The reading process is driven by two broad skill sets that are identified in the Simple View of Reading, as we have seen.

READING AND WRITING AS RECIPROCAL PROCESSES

Reading and writing are reciprocal processes (Graham, 2020) that rely on similar cognitive abilities. Allyn (2018) clearly illustrates this relationship: "Reading is like breathing in; writing is like breathing out." Cognitive abilities that provide a foundation for reading and writing include attention, verbal working memory, processing speed, and executive functioning. These cognitive abilities are closely related and share common functions (Jennings, 2022). A competent reader and writer engages in activating phonological awareness, applying sound blending to form words, decoding printed words, recognizing the word, attaching meaning, reading and writing with fluency, and comprehending the text (Jennings, 2022).

Writing is the act of placing words, sentences, and thoughts on paper. The process incorporates word recognition and reading comprehension while placing demands on verbal working memory that necessitates specific skills in mechanics, handwriting, phonology, semantics, morphology, syntax, and discourse (Jennings, 2022). Through mastery of literacy skills, students learn how to read and write, then read and write to learn academic content. Repeated exposure can occur through many different venues. Students learn through classroom discussions, presentations, hands-on activities, or other mediums, such as videos or podcasts (Sedita, 2013), as well as through writing about, reorganizing, and reflecting on these experiences. Writing is integral to learning. Writing tasks should be based on the learning experiences occurring during instruction. "Writing-to-learn means using writing tools to promote content learning; when students write, they think on paper" (Sedita, 2013, p. 2).

Reading and Writing Ropes

Scarborough (2001) created the Reading Rope to illustrate how the strands of reading are both independent and interconnected. Scarborough's rope is divided into two large strands: a language comprehension strand and a word recognition strand. The lower strand of word recognition is divided into three strands: phonological awareness, decoding, and sight recognition. The upper stand of language comprehension is divided into five strands: background knowledge, vocabulary, language structures, verbal reasoning, and literacy knowledge (Really Great Reading, 2022).

Similar to the necessity of reading skills instruction occurring in all content areas, writing too is not a single skill that develops just in the language arts classroom. Writing is composed of upper- and lower-level skills. Multiple versions of the writing rope have been created, but Carver and Pantoja (2022) have revised the rope to reflect the ways that academic writing can be used to support reading and writing growth in all content areas (see figure 1.1).

The foundational linguistic encoding process of the rope tends to begin in the primary level classroom and continues to develop throughout the K–12 experience. These lower-level processes develop and increase in automaticity, but they tend not to be addressed in secondary content instruction.

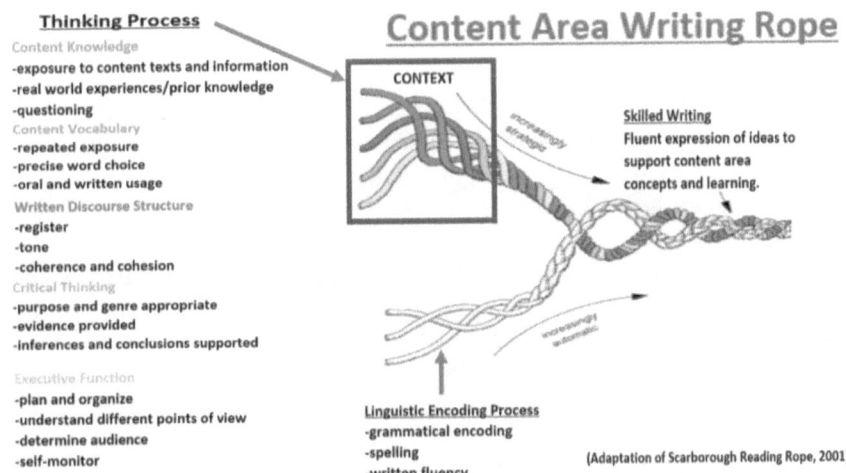

Figure 1.1 Content Area Writing Rope. (Adaption of Scarborough Reading Rope, 2001)

However, the higher-level thinking processes need to occur in specific academic contexts, so that informed writing occurs. Without this contextual basis, learners experience more difficulty processing or conveying knowledge. Content knowledge, content vocabulary, written discourse structure, critical thinking, and executive function provide the foundation for being able to express written ideas within a specific content area.

Learners increase their content knowledge through exposure to texts, lectures, videos, and presentations about the content, which typically occurs during subject specific instruction. However, learners also bring their real-world experiences and prior knowledge into the academic setting. This knowledge is expanded through teacher or student questioning. Questioning plays an integral part in learning by engaging students in the learning process and providing opportunities for inquiry. "It challenges levels of thinking and informs whether students are ready to progress with their learning. Questions that probe for deeper meaning foster critical thinking skills and higher-order capabilities such as problem-solving" (Doherty, 2017, para. 1). Questioning also occurs metacognitively through self-talk to support understanding of academic content. The process of questioning encourages the creation of critical thinkers who are able to express their ideas orally and in writing.

An understanding of specific content vocabulary is a necessary prerequisite for content area writing. Word learning is a difficult process requiring time and repeated exposures (Sinatra et al., 2012) through teacher modeling, guided, and independent practice. This repetition will help learners use the precise word choice needed to convey content area concepts. In science, writers need to know the names of specific tools such as beakers and test tubes, rather than referring to them as things or glass containers. Learners tend not to arrive in the content area classroom with an understanding of the subject specific academic vocabulary. Vocabulary instruction needs to focus on content area words as well as the meaning of prefixes, suffixes, and base and root words that are used in the specific content areas (Friedberg et al., 2017). Opportunities for both written and oral vocabulary usage are important components since oral usage often precedes written usage. Internalization of new vocabulary generally occurs once new words reach the level of being applied in the learner's writing.

Written discourse is composed of many elements. Register involves the learner's ability to determine the level and tone in which the information should be shared: formal, informal, or neutral. Formal register is generally used for professional or business writing. The informal register is more conversational. The neutral register is nonemotional and focuses on factual information that could be used in technical writing. Formal registry tends to be more rule governed than either of the other two. Some of the rules that govern formal registry are writing in the third person; avoiding slang and idioms; and the use of longer, more complex sentences (Really Learn English, 2022). Tone encompasses the writer's attitude toward the reader and the subject. The tone that is used in the writing affects how the reader will interpret its message (Ober, 1995). Coherence and cohesion in writing refer to the way a text is organized so that it flows logically. Coherence refers to the way the elements within the text are linked together to make the text semantically meaningful. Lexical cohesion refers to the meaningful relationship between sentence elements. Grammatical cohesion is the relationship between the grammatical elements within the text (Rhalmi, 2021).

Critical thinking is an important element of the writing process because it brings together the three components already discussed. An understanding of the specific genre and purpose of the written text is required for critical thinking. Writers who have an understanding of genre and purpose will be better able to determine the appropriate structure, tone, and register needed for addressing the audience through their writing. When writers express their ideas, they need to determine the appropriate genre for the written text based upon their specific goal, which can be anything from telling a story, to arguing a position, to entertaining or explaining. All of these factors will impact the organization, rhetorical devices, and linguistic features used within the written text (Dirgeyasa, 2016). Another important aspect of the written critical thinking process is finding evidence from sources to support authors' thinking about the task or topic. Finding evidence that has a true, logical, and relevant connection to the task requires a discerning mind. Not all evidence is appropriate, and without the right evidence, there will be little coherence or cohesion—important characteristics of the written discourse structure strand. Even after drawing inferences and conclusions from the evidence mined from the texts, writers must provide support, elaboration, or commentary explaining how the evidence supports their thinking. Writing is a complex process that relies heavily on students' understanding of genre and purpose and their ability to make inferences and draw conclusions after deciphering evidence in support of a topic or position.

Executive function is the culminating strand in the thinking process. It focuses on the author's ability to combine the other components into an organized project. It begins with writers' abilities to plan and organize the information to be conveyed. Authors need to understand various viewpoints on the topic to be discussed, including their own and those of others. Writers need to determine who the audience will be and how to convey ideas for that particular audience. Throughout the process, writers need to self-monitor to ensure they are conveying their ideas fluently, accurately, and in an appropriate fashion.

The lower-level skills included in the content area writing rope encompass the linguistic encoding process. These are the skills taught during the learning to write phase of writing. These begin to be developed during the Emergent and Beginning stages and become increasingly automatic as the learner matures. Grammatical encoding refers to the writer's understanding of the subject, verb, object agreement, and word order. This is further expanded to include the appropriate use of transition words and phrases (Psychology Concepts, 2022). Spelling skills develop as the learner masters encoding words containing regular and irregular spelling patterns. Written fluency refers to the learner's ability to write with a "natural flow and rhythm. Fluent writers use grade-appropriate word patterns, vocabulary, and content" (Campos, 2020, para. 1).

Stages of Reading and Writing Development

These foundational reading and writing skills are not acquired all at once but develop along a continuum through stages. These stages go by a variety of names depending on which authors you read. We identify them here as Emergent, Beginning, Transitional, Intermediate, Proficient, and Multiple Views. The developmental approach attempts to meet the learners where they are by addressing the essential literacy skills needed in that stage. Although the stages tend to build on each other, learners progress through the stages at different rates and at different ages.

The Emergent stage tends to begin during the preschool years and extends into the beginning of first grade. The age at which the stage begins depends on the exposure to reading and books in the home and during preschool experiences. It is during this stage that children learn the critical skills that pave the way for reading and writing development. During this stage, children begin to develop an interest in and enjoyment of books, expand their vocabulary, notice print, learn how to handle books, understand how words are arranged on the page, develop the ability to describe things and tell stories, explore letter knowledge, and develop phonological awareness. An Emergent writer is one who is learning to use written language and communication. Emergent writing begins with drawing, scribbling, and writing letters, and ends with conventional writing abilities. These are usually acquired in the primary grades (Strum et al., 2012).

During the Emergent stage, children derive meaning from the pictures as well as the printed text. Learners are beginning to focus more intently on the printed page. They are developing an understanding of the directionality of print and the organization of text from left to right and top to bottom. They begin to develop the concept of story and memorize favorite texts so they can "read" them independently.

The Beginning stage may appear as early as kindergarten or as late as the beginning of second grade. In the Beginning stage, learners are developing the Concept of Word. Students are developing an understanding that words have a beginning and an ending indicated by the white spaces between the words (Bowling & Cabell, 2018). They are developing phonemic awareness and the alphabetic principle, which lay the foundations for decoding and building a sight vocabulary. Their grasp of the concept of story is expanding, and they are developing an understanding of the organization of informational texts. During this stage, their writing is slow and deliberate and not particularly fluent. They are developing knowledge about simple conventions such as capitalization of initial words and using ending punctuation (Gehsmann & Templeton, 2022).

The Transitional stage generally appears during first grade and may continue through second or third grade. During the Transitional stage, learners are increasing their reading and writing rate, accuracy, and expression. With the increase in the number of sight words, children are moving from read alouds to becoming silent readers. During this stage, children are better able to analyze, generalize, and summarize based on their own reading (Madura, 1998). Their writing is progressing as well. They are able to focus more extensively on ideas and are more aware of the purpose and the audience for their writing (Gehsmann & Templeton, 2022).

The Intermediate stage becomes more evident by third grade and continues through fourth and fifth grades. During this stage, students are developing their ability to sustain attention over longer texts and periods of time (Mills et al., 2018). Through this expanded wide reading, students are dramatically increasing their vocabulary acquisition and their understanding of Greek and Latin morphemes. These learners are incorporating the more complex features of the narrative and informational texts to which they are exposed. Because of more fluent encoding and decoding, writing becomes a method to support learning as well as to respond to learning (Gehsmann & Templeton, 2022).

As students move into the middle school years, they tend to be ready to enter the Proficient stage, where they are beginning to understand multiple viewpoints (Chall, 1983). They are developing the ability to be more strategic and flexible with their strategy use as they analyze themes and motivation of characters. Knowledge of Greek and Latin roots and word etymology is becoming more important. Learners are beginning to read and write using more sophisticated, discipline-specific vocabulary.

Chall's last stage of reading development of Construction and Reconstruction (Chall, 1983) is reached during the high school and college years. Readers and writers are using print and written means to convey information from multiple viewpoints to inform, persuade, and entertain. During this stage, readers are making their own decisions about what to read and what not to read. Readers and writers make informed, selective use of material in their central areas of concern.

ANTICIPATION GUIDE REVISITED

At the beginning of the chapter, you examined four statements. Based upon what you have read in this chapter, revisit the anticipation guide statements and decide if your views are the same or have changed.

1. Literacy encompasses the same skills it did 50 years ago.
2. Reading and writing are reciprocal skills.
3. Balanced literacy and structured literacy are the same thing.
4. With the increased emphasis on literacy instruction, students' mean literacy scores on national assessments are improving.

CONCLUSION

Literacy encompasses reading and writing, but it is certainly not limited to these two processes. Literacy involves reading, writing, listening, viewing, and speaking. Literacy is a tool for meaningful engagement with others. As we move into a digital world, this ability becomes even more important (NCTE, 2020).

Reading and writing acquisition is a developmental process that occurs in stages. However, as children progress through each of the stages, there is not necessarily a smooth transition from one stage to another. Students explore texts and words at their present level of understanding in their zone of proximal development while applying their knowledge to texts and words in the next stage. Instruction needs to be targeted across the stages, so that the learner has multiple opportunities to interact with text at one level while preparing to move to another level. If instruction is just focused on the next level, learners can become frustrated, which will delay growth (Templeton, 2020).

Table 1.1 Activities for Literacy Approaches

Approach	Example Activities
Whole language	
Systematic phonics	
Structured literacy	
Balanced literacy	
Simple view of reading	
Active view of reading	

STOP AND THINK

1. Examine the instructional practices evident in your classroom. Identify examples from each of the approaches in a table similar to table 1.1. After identifying activities, indicate which approach is used most frequently in your instruction.
2. Describe the stages of reading and writing instruction. Decide which stage encompasses the majority of the students in your classroom. Provide specific examples of the characteristics that support your observation.

REFERENCES

Allyn, P. (2018, Dec. 4). Reading is like breathing in; Writing is like breathing out. *EDU Scholastic's blog abut education and learning.* https://edublog.scholastic.com/post/reading-breathing-writing-breathing-out

Bowling, E. C. C., & Cabell, S. Q. (2018, June 20). Developing readers: Understanding concept of word in text development in emergent readers. *Early Childhood Education Journal.* https://doi.org/10.1007/s10643-018-0902-1

Campos, M. (2022). Seven effective strategies to build writing fluency. EnglishPost.org. https://englishpost.org/strategies-build-writing-fluency/

Carter, D. (2016, September 7). How has literacy changed in 50 years? *ProLiteracy.* https://www.proliteracy.org/Blogs/Article/138/How-Has-Literacy-Changed-in-50-Years#:~:text=In%20the%20past%2050%20years,number%20is%20less%20than%2010%25

Carver, L., & Pantoja, L. (2022). Writing-to-learn. In H. S. Atkins & L. Carver (Eds.), *Writing is thinking: Strategies for all content areas* (pp. 1–15). Rowman & Littlefield.

Chall, J. (1983). *Stages of reading development.* McGraw Hill.

Dirgeyasa, I. W. (2016). Genre-based approach: What and how to teach and learn writing. https://files.eric.ed.gov/fulltext/EJ1107874.pdf

Doherty, J. (2017, July 9). Skillful questioning: The beating heart of good pedagogy. *Impact.* https://my.chartered.college/impact_article/skilful-questioning-the-beating-heart-of-good-pedagogy/

Duke, N. K., & Cartwright, K. B. (2021, May). The science of reading progresses: Communicating advances beyond the simple view of reading. *Reading Research Quarterly, 56*(S1), S25–S44. https://doi.org/10.1002/rrg.411

Farrell, L., Hunter, M., Davidson, M., & Osenga, T. (2019). The simple view of reading. Reading Rockets. https://www.readingrockets.org/article/simple-view-reading

Friedberg, C., Mitchell, A., & Brooke, E. (2017). Understanding academic language and its connection to school success. Lexia Learning. https://www.lexialearning.com/sites/default/files/resources/Whitepaper_Understanding_Academic_Language.pdf

Gehsmann, K., & Templeton, S. (2022). *Teaching reading and writing: The developmental approach* (2nd ed.). Pearson.

Gough, P. E., & Tunmer, W. E. (1986). Decoding, reading, and reading disability. *Remedial and Special Education, 7*(1), 6–10. https://doi.org/10.1177/074193258600700104

Graham, S. (2020). The science of reading and writing must become more fully integrated. *Reading Research Quarterly, 55*(S1), S35–S44.

Hoover, W. A., & Tunmer, W. E. (2020). *The cognitive foundations of reading and its acquisition.* Springer.

Jennings, T. (2022). The relationship between reading and writing: An overview. Lexicon Reading Center. https://www.lexiconreadingcenter.org/reading-and-writing-relationships-an-overview/

LeBlanc, C. (2021, October 14). Nation's Report Card shows historic declines in reading, math scores. Fatherly. https://www.fatherly.com/news/nations-report-card-test-scores-naep-math-reading-decline

Lorimor-Easley, N. A., & Reed, D. K. (2019, April 9). An explanation of structure literacy, and a comparison to balanced literacy. Iowa Reading Research Center. https://iowareadingresearch.org/blog/structured-and-balanced-literacy

Madura, S. (1998). *Transitional readers and writers respond to literature through discussion, writing, and art* [Unpublished doctoral dissertation]. University of Nevada.

Mills, K. A., Stornaiuolo, A., Smith, A., & Pandya, J. (2018). *Handbook of writing, literacies, and education in digital cultures.* Routledge.

National Council of Teachers of English (NCTE). (2020). Literacy is more than just reading and writing. https://ncte.org/blog/2020/03/literacy-just-reading-writing/

Ober, S. (1995). *Contemporary Business Communication.* (2nd ed.). Houghton Mifflin.

Ordetx, K. (2021, January 14). What is the science of reading? *IMSE Journal.* https://journal.imse.com/what-is-the-science-of-reading/

Pilgrim, J., & Martinez, E. (2013). Defining literacy in the 21st century: A guide to terminology and skills. *Texas Journal of Literacy Education, 1*(1), 60–69. https://files.eric.ed.gov/fulltext/EJ1110822.pdf

Psychology Concepts. (2020). Linguistic coding. http://psychologyconcepts.com/linguistic-encoding/

Reading Horizons. (2022). Reading wars: Phonics vs. whole language instruction. https://www.readinghorizons.com/reading-strategies/teaching/phonics-instruction/reading-wars-phonics-vs-whole-language-reading-instruction

Really Great Reading. (2022). What is Scarborough's reading rope? https://www.reallygreatreading.com/content/scarboroughs-reading-rope

Really Learn English. (2022). Learn English vocabulary and easy English Grammar. https://www.really-learn-english.com/

Rhalmi, M. (2021). The difference between coherence and cohesion? https://www.myenglishpages.com/blog/difference-between-coherence-and-cohesion/

Scarborough, H. S. (2001). Connecting early language and literacy to later reading (dis)abilities: Evidence, theory, and practice. In S. Neuman & D. Dickinson (Eds.), *Handbook for research in early literacy* (pp. 97–110). Guilford Press.

Sedita, J. (2013). Learning to write and writing-to-learn. In M. C. Hougen (Ed.), *Fundamentals of literacy instruction and assessment: 6–12* (pp. 97–114). Paul H. Brookes. https://keystoliteracy.com/wp-content/uploads/2012/08/Learning%20to%20Write%20and%20Writing%20to%20Learn.pdf

Sinatra, R., Zygouris-Coe, V., & Dasinger, S. B. (2012): Preventing a vocabulary lag: What lessons are learned from research, *Reading & Writing Quarterly: Overcoming Learning Difficulties*, 28(4), 333-357. https://www.tandfonline.com/doi/abs/10.1080/10573569.2012.702040?journalCode=urwl20

Sinclair, L. F. (2017). Relationship of literacy to income, employability, and performance: A quantitative analysis. ProQuest. https://www.proquest.com/openview/519dd655a58efa869081f61b54153692/1?pq-origsite=gscholar&cbl=18750&diss=y

Spear-Swerling, L. (2015). Common Types of Reading Problems and How to Help Children Who Have Them. *The Reading Teacher*, 69(5), 513-522. doi:10.1002/trtr.1410

Strum, J. M., Cali, K., Nelson, M., & Staskowski, M. (2012, October). The developmental writing scale: A new progress monitoring tool for beginning writers. *Topics in Language Disorders*, 32(4), 297–318. https://doi.org.10.1097/TLD.0b013e318272159e

Templeton, S. (2020). Stages, phases, repertoires, and waves: Learning to spell and read words. *The Reading Teacher*, 74(3), 315–323.

U.S. Department of Education. (1999). *Literacy in the labor force: Results from the National Adult Literacy Survey*. National Center for Education Statistics. https://nces.ed.gov/pubs99/1999470.pdf

Wagner, T. (2010). *The global achievement gap*. Basic Books.

Chapter 2

Emergent Stage

Gretchen Rudolph-Fladd and Lin Carver

It is the start of the reading block, and Mrs. Aultman has chosen *No, David!* (Shannon, 1998) for the read aloud to her class of kindergarteners. She gathers them on the carpet in front of her rocking chair and slowly reveals the cover of her book. Many of the students share remarks of joy; perhaps the book has been read to them before, others may connect to the childlike drawings that are full of color, and some may just be happy because they love having books read to them. Mrs. Aultman knows that reading aloud is one of the most powerful keys to developing the literacy process for her young students while also building comprehension and language. She is also cognizant that talking about the text while she reads scaffolds the learning of her struggling readers and provides additional meaning for her higher readers (Allyn & Morrell, 2016).

Before reading, Mrs. Aultman asks the students to predict what they think the book will be about. While she completes the picture walk, she shows all of the colorful pictures and enjoys having her students share the comments about some of the messes David has made. She knows the most effective read aloud is one that involves students asking and answering questions (McGee & Schickendanz, 2007). Mrs. Aultman then begins to read, pausing on each page, asking her students probing questions, and allowing them to share their responses to the story.

ANTICIPATION GUIDE

Before reading this chapter, read the following four statements. As you read the statements, determine if you agree or disagree with them. Then read the chapter. After completing the chapter, you will decide if your original thoughts have changed.

1. Children master oral language outside of the classroom setting; it can't be addressed in the classroom setting.
2. Key predictors of success for early literacy are alphabetic code, oral language, print concepts, and rhyming.
3. Phonological awareness and phonemic awareness are the same thing.
4. Telling stories with pictures is part of Emergent reading skills.

CHARACTERISTICS OF EMERGENT READERS

Emergent readers must accomplish significant work prior to developing conventional reading skills. Reading is not simply a way to move through levels and word lists. Instead, young children must be given time to cultivate meaning, foster a positive disposition toward reading, and develop strong reading identities before they ever begin decoding (Collins & Glover, 2015). During the Emergent stage, readers begin to identify letters; they understand that writing letters can create a message, they scribble or make marks to imitate writing, and they begin to recognize words or letters from their environment, such as the letters of their names or the word "STOP." According to the National Center for Family Literacy (2009), five skills are moderately correlated with success in later literacy achievement:

- print concepts such as identifying the book, cover, author, left to right, and front to back, etc.;
- print knowledge, which encompasses alphabetic knowledge, print concepts, and early decoding;
- reading readiness, which includes the print concepts and knowledge listed previously, as well as vocabulary and early decoding skills;
- oral language skills, which include the understanding and ability to produce and comprehend the spoken language, including vocabulary and grammar; and
- visual processing, which is the ability to match or identify symbols.

During the Emergent reading stage, students identify words by memorizing their visual symbols or by guessing the meaning from context. They also begin to recognize some letters of the alphabet and use them within context to remember words by sight (Ehri, 1999).

ROLE OF ORAL LANGUAGE

Oral language development during preschool and kindergarten is key to early literacy acquisition, which provides the foundation for conventional reading success. Oral language skills are comprised of expressive and receptive vocabulary and syntactic knowledge, as well as narrative dialoguing processes that include both comprehension and storytelling. Oral language skills contribute to success in decoding skills, thus allowing the developing comprehension skills to become evident (Whorrall & Cabell, 2015).

The child's linguistic environment impacts later oral language development (Whorrall & Cabell, 2015). Decades of research have highlighted the discrepancy in achievement between young children who live in poverty and those in more affluent settings, as a result of fewer opportunities for exposure to oral language. This oral language gap has been estimated to be as large as 32 million words by the age of four (Hart & Risley, 1995). Purposeful conversations that incorporate complex vocabulary words and open-ended questions connect to students' interests and challenge critical thinking skills, which support the development of oral language skills, especially in preschool and kindergarten classes (Whorrall & Cabell, 2015).

CONCEPT OF WORD

Typically, the Concept of Word in text has focused on understanding the match between speech and print, but it is more than this basic skill. A solid Concept of Word in text is actually the culmination of automatic knowledge of letter sounds, the ability to isolate beginning consonant sounds, and the ability to remember words in isolation that have been seen in other places. Incorporating Concept of Word instruction into daily literacy education will not only strengthen students' speech-to-print match, but it will also develop their alphabetical knowledge, phonemic awareness, and knowledge of words in print (Blackwell-Bullock et al., n.d.).

Only when children understand that words are composed of individual sounds that can be changed to form new words, and the impact of changing phonemes within the word, are they able to master the letter and sound relationships. These letter and sound relationships provide the foundation for the Emergent stage of reading and writing. Emergent writing may begin with a picture, scribbles, or just a single letter representing an entire word, such as "b" for "ball." As students learn to extend and identify the ending sounds in words, they may add the letter "l" to the "b" as they attempt to encode the word. The use of inventive spellings may help learners to develop a stronger sense of phonemic awareness as part of their early literacy skills (Cunningham, 2013).

It is important to note that even children who have had reading and writing experiences before they enter kindergarten may not be able to read common words, such as "the," "of," or "and." Instead, they most likely have a solid understanding of approximately ten concrete words that are important to them. For example, a girl named Ellie may know "Ellie," "Mom," "Dad," "Beau" (her brother), "I love you" (often viewed as one word), "Iesa" (her grandmother), "Papa" (her grandfather), "McDonald's," "Gracie" (her dog), and "Finn" (her cat). Reading these words is important, not because they represent a mastery of reading those ten words, but because they illustrate an achievement of a fundamental understanding: knowing how to learn words (Cunningham, 2013).

PHONOLOGICAL AWARENESS

Phonological awareness is the broad term that incorporates the ability to distinguish between the sounds of the language, including separating sentences into words, words into syllables, and syllables into parts. Phonological awareness is not a single skill; rather, it develops through a progression of stages. First, children learn that language consists of individual words; next, they develop skills in rhyming and alliteration. After they understand that words are composed of syllables, they then master onset and rime manipulation, and finally, they progress to phonemic awareness (Moats & Tolman, 2009). Phonemic awareness refers to the ability to recognize and manipulate discrete sounds or phonemes within a word. Phonological awareness is a skill that can be taught and is promoted by intentional application of instructional approaches and strategies (Smith et al., 1998).

Young children are not learning the terminology within the phonemic and phonological awareness strands; rather, they are demonstrating the ability to perform these tasks. For example, children might not be able to convey that "Florida" has three syllables and "fish" has one, but they can clap out three beats for "Florida" and one for "fish." They may not be able to identify the first phoneme in "bat" is represented by the grapheme "b"; however, they can distinguish the difference between the first sound in "bat" and the first sound in "cat" (Cunningham, 2013).

Rhyming

A basic phonological awareness skill is rhyming words. Children who understand the concept of rhyming are able to hear and say rhyming words. Rhyme is distinguished by the "acoustic agreement of sounds made of vowels and consonants and is associated with the phonological and phonetic system of language" (Grofcikova & Macajova, 2021, p. 6). Children who struggle to rhyme often focus on the first and last sounds of the word or the meaning of the word, rather than understanding that a rhyme focuses on the rime portion of the word. The most basic way to teach children how to rhyme is through the use of nursery rhymes. Nursery rhymes appeal to young children because of the intonation, rhythmic quality, entertainment, and fantasy components (Grofcikova & Macajova, 2021). Preschool and kindergarten classrooms should be filled with nursery rhymes. Children should be encouraged to recite, sing, act out, and clap out these rhymes (Cunningham, 2013).

Syllables

Once children have an understanding that speech is a compilation of words, they are equipped to separate words into component parts. Just like most skills, auditory discrimination is a learned skill. Identifying the number of syllables in a word is often one of the first skills taught. Clapping is the most common method for teaching children how to identify syllables in words (Cunningham, 2013).

Syllabication is an auditory discrimination skill. Emergent readers can listen for syllables within words by beating on a xylophone or using maracas. Students can also make tapping motions in the air, or snap, pat, or stomp to represent each of the syllables. Learners who are experiencing difficulty determining the number of syllables in a word can put their hands under their chins when saying a specific word. This way they are able to determine the syllables by counting the number of times their chins drop, using kinesthetic cues in addition to auditory cues. Children develop the understanding that in order to form a syllable, they need to open their mouths. So, counting the number of times their chin drops helps the students focus their attention on the important information to develop those auditory discrimination skills (Tankersley, 2003).

When children are able to determine the number of beats or syllables in a word, they begin to make a correlation between one-beat words as short words and three-beat words as longer words. This correlation transfers to writing, encouraging students to use more letters for words that contain more beats (Cunningham, 2013).

PHONEMIC AWARENESS

Phonemic awareness is the last stage in the phonological continuum, but it actually encompasses many skills. When learners have developed phonemic awareness, they recognize words that rhyme and they can distinguish similar beginning phonemes, such as in the words "car" and "cat." They can isolate the three sounds in a word such as "cat" and say them individually. "The best predictor of reading difficulty in kindergarten or first grade is the inability to segment words and syllables into constituent sound units (phonemic awareness)" (Lyon, 1995, p. 3).

Emergent readers learn to distinguish between the phonemes, or the smallest sounds that compose spoken language. In the English language there are 44 phonemes that can be combined to make syllables and words. Phonemic awareness is the ability to focus on and manipulate phonemes in oral language. Emergent readers need to be taught to isolate, identify, categorize, blend, segment, and delete these phonemes. Students can then be taught to manipulate onsets, the single consonant or blend that comes before the vowel, and rimes, the vowel and consonant that follow the onset (Ehri et al., 2001). Phonemic awareness is highly correlated to the success of Beginning readers (National Reading Panel, 2000).

Phonemic awareness instruction typically occurs over a span of two to three years, during kindergarten and first to second grade. Kindergarten instruction should encompass rhyming, word matching beginning sounds, and blending sounds into words. First-grade instruction progresses to more advanced instruction, including a focus on blending, segmentation, substitution, and manipulation of phonemes. Phonemic awareness skills should follow a scope and sequence that allows the skills to increase in difficulty (University of Oregon, n.d.).

Phonemic awareness typically begins with the easiest skills of syllable segmentation and blending in compound words. This ability is followed by onset-rime blending and segmentation and blending and segmentation of individual phonemes. Finally, instruction is provided in phoneme deletion and manipulation of initial consonants and blends, final consonants and blends, and medial sounds. This final stage may develop as late as at seven to nine years of age (Moats & Tolman, 2009).

Onset-Rime

Syllables are composed of onsets and rimes. The onset is the beginning phonological unit, which is composed of an initial consonant or a consonant blend portion of a syllable before the vowel. The rime is the group of letters that follows the onset, typically containing a vowel and any final consonants. For example, in the word "bat," "b" is the onset and "at" is the rime. When young children understand onset and rime, combined with rhyming, they are able to build an awareness of the most common parts of words. Through instruction in word families, children develop a basis for decoding that supports automaticity and benefits both spelling and writing. Decoding is learned through blending and segmenting the onset and rime of words and word families (Lynch, 2021a).

DEVELOPING CONCEPTS OF PRINT

At the same time that Emergent readers are developing auditory skills, they are developing visual skills as well. Print awareness, a visual skill, is the understanding that written language is connected to oral language. When young children lack print awareness, they are unlikely to become strong readers. Print awareness is one of the early predictors of reading success, and it does not occur naturally. Rather, print awareness develops through active interaction between adults and children, in which letters, words, and other print features are discussed frequently. It occurs as a result of being read to, playing with letters, engaging in word games, and finally through formal reading instruction (Texas Education Agency, 2002).

When print awareness has developed, children are able to understand how the system of print functions. They begin by learning that print provides a message. They master book concepts that include an awareness that books are read from top to bottom and front to back, as well as titles, authors, illustrators, and short synopses that tell the reader about the book. Print concepts also include knowledge of directionality. Students learn to identify the front and back of the book and how to turn the pages from front to back. They realize that lines of print are read from left to right and from top to bottom. Return sweep is an important skill mastered during the Emergent stage. Children learn that they read across the line from left to right and then sweep back to the beginning left-hand side of the text line that follows (Victoria State Government, 2020).

Finally, learners also grasp the mechanics of print. They develop the understanding that words are separated by a white space and the ability to differentiate between the various types of symbols: letters, numbers, and punctuation. Emergent readers realize the role that capitalization and punctuation play in print. They understand the stability of the letter-sound relationship and realize that printed words will always be read in the same manner (Victoria State Government, 2020).

Environmental Print

Almost half a century of research has shown that environmental print has an early influence on literacy skills. Children's early interactions with environmental print are their first exposure to the written language. These exposures teach children that abstract symbols have meaning. When children first begin reading environmental print, they start by recognizing labels or logos that are associated with words. As their knowledge of print and phonics skills grow, young children begin to read words and separate them from the labels or logos (Giles & Tunk, 2010). Environmental print expose students not only to early reading experiences, but also to early writing experiences. Children who are exposed to environmental print begin to engage with environmental printing, using it in three ways: (1) copying with no understanding of the word's meaning, (2) using it as a resource for correct spellings of words within a message, or (3) inspiring a writing topic (Tunk & Giles, 2007).

Function of Letters

Letter identification occurs when children can name letters, identify their characteristics, and know the formation for 26 uppercase and lowercase letter symbols, totaling 52 (or 54 if both possible representations for "g" and "a" are included). Letter identification is key to early literacy and should not be minimized. Letter identification ranks among one of the top predictors of reading success when compared to other early reading skills (Adolph et al., 2010). Letter identification fluency exists when students can find and say letters and their names both in and out of context, not just with accuracy but also with automaticity. When children learn letters and play with letters, it increases their interest in sounds and reading. This early interaction allows children to see and hear the auditory link between letter names and their sounds, effectively providing background knowledge for phonemic awareness and letter identification, as well as other phonics skills (Lynch, 2020).

CHARACTERISTICS OF TEXT FOR EMERGENT READERS

Emergent readers are gaining an understanding that the purpose of print is to communicate. Teachers of Emergent readers know the value of reading a variety of books to their learners. Both teacher read alouds and shared readings are important. Read alouds can improve comprehension, increase vocabulary, and model fluency (Okello, 2021). Shared reading occurs when the teacher and student read a book together. A book chosen for shared reading is usually read together multiple times. Big books and predictable pattern books are perfect for shared reading. Teachers begin by reading most of the book aloud to the students. As the students begin to recognize the pattern, they join in the reading. Predictable patterns allow students to enjoy the repeated refrains, patterns, and pictures. Pretend reading is a key stage that all children experience with a favorite book that an adult has read to them many times. Children learn what reading is from pretend reading. They develop confidence and print concepts, as well as an understanding of letter and sound relationships (Cunningham, 2013).

Shared reading allows children to start by pretending to read and then move into reading of predictable texts. Learners are also exposed to vocabulary, story structure, and content knowledge through involvement with teacher read alouds (Tompkins, 2017).

CHARACTERISTICS OF EMERGENT WRITERS

Emergent writers begin by using scribbles to represent writing. While these markings at first appear to be randomly placed on the page, as children gain experience with writing, they begin to line up their letters or drawings from left to right and top to bottom. They also begin to tell the stories their pictures represent, which is the first demonstration of their reading. When they first begin telling the story of their writing, they may only be able to remember directly after drawing; however, once children gain experience, they will learn to remember what their drawings depict, and as their writing becomes more conventional, they will be able to better decipher it. At this point, students begin to distinguish between writing and drawing (Tompkins, 2017).

Emergent writers may also dictate stories for their teachers to write for them. This process helps students understand that their speech can be recorded. It also provides learners with a model illustrating the left to right and top to bottom arrangement of print on the page. Emergent writers typically can write their first and last names, up to 20 high-frequency words, and use sentence frames to write a sentence (Tompkins, 2017).

INSTRUCTIONAL METHODS FOR EMERGENT READERS

When teaching Emergent literacy skills, it is critical to use instructional methods that are supported by research. Emergent readers are not all alike; some will acquire foundational skills easily, while others will struggle, which is why it is important to differentiate in Emergent classrooms. Teachers must use direct, explicit instruction that includes explanations, modeling, and guided practice. Systematic phonological awareness must be incorporated with plenty of practice time for students to distinguish and manipulate sounds. Instruction should begin with the simplest subset of this skill, which is rhyming, and move into the most complex phoneme manipulation (Hamman, 2019).

In addition to direct, explicit instruction, teaching Emergent readers and writers requires teachers to use many of the instructional practices that are employed with older beginning and fluent readers. Teachers should use read alouds; guided reading with decodable and leveled books; instruction from basal readers; and time for student-selected, independent reading and writing. The key difference is that preschool and kindergarten teachers scaffold these instructional practices to allow young children to experience success (Tompkins, 2017).

In order for students to develop strong foundational reading and writing skills, they must have plenty of practice opportunities that are presented in strategic ways. First, these learners need practice with print concepts that include letter recognition, handwriting, and an understanding of books. Next, students need instruction in phonological awareness that includes general listening, rhyming, blending and segmenting syllables, identifying onset-rime, isolating, blending and segmenting phonemes, and manipulating and deleting phonemes (Achieve the Core, n.d.).

After phonological awareness, learners need to be immersed in phonics and word recognition instruction, which includes letter-sound identification, decoding, and encoding. Emergent readers are working on recognizing letters and the sounds they represent in text, high-frequency words, and decodable words. Throughout all of these phases, students need opportunities to practice fluency (Achieve the Core, n.d.). Instructional practices for Emergent readers can occur through wordless books, predictable pattern books, nursery rhymes, rhyming picture books, or a favorite read aloud they have heard multiple times.

USING TEXTS WITH EMERGENT READERS

Emergent readers should be immersed in text. Their classrooms should be rich in labels, environmental print, and traditional print materials. Literacy materials should be available in centers within these preschool and kindergarten classrooms. Big books, predictable texts, and poems and rhymes on charts should be used during shared reading (Tompkins, 2017).

In addition to books, early literacy classrooms should have magazines and newspapers. There should be charts with recipes and directional reminders for students. The classroom should have labels for objects, areas, and students' names. Word walls can provide support for young children as they associate meaning with more difficult words (Tompkins, 2017).

Effective word walls are selective and limited to common words students use frequently. No more than five or six words should be added to the word wall each week, and to emphasize its value the teacher needs to frequently refer to the wall throughout the day. Bulletin boards should be rich in content vocabulary and labels for pictures should be related to concepts students are learning. Children's drawings and writings should be displayed to emphasize that all writing is important (Cunningham, 2013).

WORDLESS BOOKS

Wordless books are books in which an entire story is told completely through the illustrations (Tompkins, 2017). These books are powerful tools to be used for early literacy development. They engage children, allow them to make predictions, require critical thinking skills, and provide meaning and a story-telling opportunity (Burnett, 2018). Wordless books help students understand the basic elements of a story: plot, characters, and setting (Tompkins, 2017).

Pancakes for Breakfast (dePaola, 1978) is a great book for young readers to illustrate how determination can lead to the desired outcome. Children will enjoy the humor as the little old lady hunts for ingredients to make her pancakes. Students will easily identify the cold, winter morning when they see the snow on the title page. They will also recognize that the little old lady lives on a farm because she gathers eggs from her chickens and milks her cows, and that it may take time to gather additional ingredients from either a store or a neighbor (dePaola, 1978).

Picture Walk

An interactive read aloud is an effective strategy to enhance comprehension through engaging students in a picture walk and a discussion. The teacher introduces the book by activating background knowledge before beginning the book. With *Pancakes for Breakfast* (dePaola, 1978), before reading the teacher can ask students to look at the picture on the cover and compare that to what they like to eat for breakfast. Next, the teacher engages students during reading by pausing and asking questions about the pictures and encouraging students to engage in a conversation related to focusing on details, which is the skill being taught.

The teacher asks the students about the setting, having them focus on details from the pictures that allow them to draw conclusions. For example, the pictures of the cat and the dog on the cover can help students determine that the woman likes pets, or the large stack of pancakes can help them determine that the woman is very hungry. Timing is key with this step; the teacher needs to know when it is more effective to stop to allow students to identify important details, to clarify confusion, or to predict the conclusion. After reading the book, it is critical to have students respond to the story (Tompkins, 2017).

Point around the Picture

After reading *Pancakes for Breakfast* (dePaola, 1978), the teacher can ask the class to think about what they like to eat for breakfast. The students can create their own pictures to illustrate their own favorite breakfast foods. Using the writing strategy point around the picture, children can verbalize and elaborate on details in their own wordless pictures (Serravallo, 2017). With this strategy each student points to one portion of their illustration and elaborates on the part of the picture where their finger landed (Serravallo, 2017). At first the students may need prompting with questions such as "What is for breakfast?" "Where are you sitting?" "Is this at home or a restaurant?" It is important to encourage the child to include as many details as possible. These pictures can be shared individually with the teacher, in small groups with peers, or with the whole class.

PREDICTABLE PATTERN BOOKS

Children learn concepts of print and oral language through exposure to books. At the Emergent stage, even before children know that letters are print and that there is a relationship between the two, children benefit from predictable pattern books. When teachers read books that have rhythmic patterned language, children begin to see that each word on the page stands for a specific spoken word. This connection allows students to understand that speech is composed of separate parts, which is a key component in understanding the reading process. These predictable books are appropriate for Emergent readers because they do not require students to have mastered the alphabetic principle (Beech, 2005).

Leader and Chorus Choral Reading

Brown Bear, Brown Bear (Martin, 1967) is perfect for the leader and chorus choral reading strategy because of the repeated phrases throughout the story. This whole group reading activity allows students to practice oral reading and learn how to read expressively and fluently. There are several choral reading arrangements that can be implemented, but they are always most effectively used after the teacher has first modeled the book. Rather than having students repeat each line, the leader and chorus strategy calls for the leader to read the main part and the group to read the refrain chorally (Tompkins, 2017).

For this book, the leader would read "Brown bear, brown bear" and the class would read the line "What do you see?" and the line "Looking at me." This can be extended to have one student recite the first phrase or sentence, and then another student recites the repeated phrases (Tompkins, 2017). It is key for the leader to point to the words as the line is read. The teacher can also call on one student to point to words as the class reads the choral line.

Remembering to incorporate Concept of Word instruction into all daily literacy activities is critical (Blackwell-Bullock et al., n.d.), as Emergent readers develop understanding at different times. While many children may already possess knowledge of words in print, never miss an opportunity to practice these skills.

Predictable Charts

This leader-chorus echo reading strategy complements the writing strategy predictable charts because the students will continue to focus on lines from the book. When using predictable charts, teachers and students collaboratively write numerous sentences using the same sentence stem. For this book, the teacher would begin by writing the first sentence of the book on a chart: "Brown bear, brown bear, what do you see?" The class could together decide on a possible answer to the question, with the teacher acting as the scribe to write the answer. In this way the class can create their own version of the book *Brown Bear, Brown Bear*. Once the class has completed their new book, children can read the story by pointing to each word (Cunningham, 2013).

NURSERY RHYMES

The ability to recite nursery rhymes is one of the best indicators of future reading proficiency for children who enter kindergarten (Slater, 2002). Understanding and making rhyming words is a key skill in the phonemic awareness continuum. Nursery rhymes, as well as other rhyming books, are great tools for developing vocabulary, phonological awareness, and the concept of rhyme and alliteration, along with fine and gross motor skills. Early childhood educators should involve children in reciting, clapping, acting out, and singing rhymes (Bennett, 2019). Once children are able to perform all of those skills with rhymes, they are ready to explore the concept of rhyming in their literacy instruction (Cunningham, 2013).

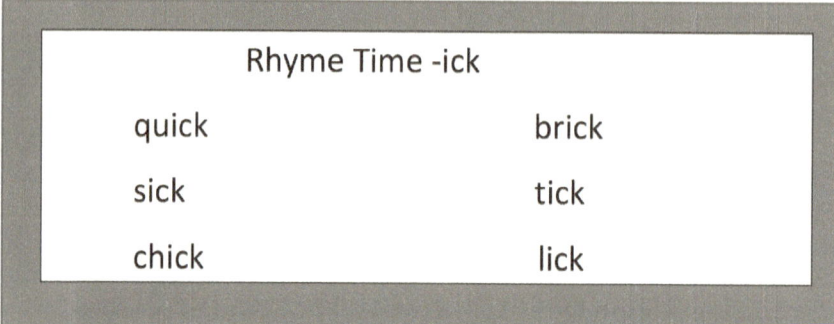

Figure 2.1 Rhyme Time

Rhyming

Jack Be Nimble (Stewart, 2004) is a nursery rhyme that could be used at the beginning of the school year. The teacher reads the first six lines of the poem to the class. Using this rhyme, oral vocabulary can be expanded through a discussion of the meaning of the words "nimble" and "spry." The second time the teacher reads the poem, the class uses large motor skills to depict the poem while the teacher reads it. After the second reading, the class picks out words that end with similar rhyming sounds. There are three sets of rhyming words in this poem: "quick" and "candlestick," "spry" and "pie," and "high" and "sky." The class could be divided in half. The first half recites the line but stops before the last rhyming word. The other half of the class waits for the pause and then recites the rhyming word (Cunningham, 2013).

Rhyme Time

After practicing the concept of rhyme, students can practice writing rhyming words. The teacher can use the strategy rhyme time to help students generate a list of words that rhyme with "quick." The teacher creates a chart labeled Rhyme Time at the top and places "-ick" at the top of the chart (Serravallo, 2017) (see figure 2.1).

Students can work together to generate a list of words for the teacher to write on the chart. After the students have completed the rhyme time chart, they can paste a picture to represent each word. The teacher underlines the "-ick" ending in the first word, then she has students underline the matching "-ick" portion they see in each word (Serravallo, 2017).

RHYMING BOOKS

Once students have mastered the ability to recite nursery rhymes and generate rhyming word lists, the use of more complex rhyming picture books can help learners write their own rhyming sentences. *Llama Llama Red Pajama* (Dewdney, 2005) is a great story to reinforce rhyming, but it also can be used to help develop comprehension skills. Comprehension instruction should not wait until Intermediate grades; instruction should begin with our youngest learners (Reed, 2016).

Describing Characters

The main character in *Llama Llama Red Pajama* provides an effective way to focus on obvious character traits using the strategy describing characters. After sharing the story as a read aloud, the teacher draws a picture of Llama on chart paper. Then the students describe the main character. The teacher writes simple words or symbols on sticky notes and adds them to the picture as the students share characteristics. This chart and set of sticky notes can then be added to a center where students can reread the book and place the sticky notes on pages where the specific characteristics are evident (Linder, 2014). To provide students with independent time to process character traits, they should be given blank sheets of paper to draw their own pictures of Llama showing their favorite characteristic.

Share the Pen

After reading *Llama Llama Red Pajama* (Dewdney, 2005), the teacher can use the share the pen writing strategy. This strategy allows all students to respond to text even if they do not yet have fully developed writing skills. Emergent writers are ready to write, but they are not always able to write in a conventional way because they are still learning to form letters. While letter-writing skills are important, even students who have not mastered these skills need opportunities to express their ideas on paper (Nikol, 2021).

ABC BOOKS

Alphabet books are primarily written for young children to learn how to identify the letters of the alphabet, but they can also be used to teach the concepts of print (Tompkins, 2017). Emergent readers enjoy alphabet books because the structure is familiar. They like to see what person, place, or thing the author chooses for each letter, especially for letters like "X" or "Q" because these letters are harder to find words to represent their sounds. Some alphabet books are simple and easy for children to read, using the pictures as a resource for the letter, while others can be centered around a more complex topic and use the alphabet to share information. Consequently, these texts can be used to span the Emergent, Beginning, and Transitional stages of literacy development (Barone, 2010).

Alphabet knowledge is a component of the concepts of print. Alphabet books encourage literacy development by helping students unlock symbols of the language, connect knowledge to other sources, support the acquisition of book orientation knowledge, provide enjoyment, and help young children develop independence in both reading and writing (Warner & Weiss, 2005).

Concepts of Print

F Is for Florida (Farley & Miles, 2018) is not only an effective text that can be used for children to learn about print concepts, but it also helps to expand students' knowledge about the state of Florida. When reading the book aloud, the teacher can focus on letter recognition, locating upper- and lowercase letters within the text, rhyming words on each page, and vocabulary development. The three to four lines of print on each page make this text particularly appropriate for teaching concepts of print, including book orientation; directionality of print; knowledge of the alphabetic system; and the distinction between sentences, words, and letters (Victoria State Government, 2020). The teacher can help students find differences between letters and words, noticing that the alphabet letters in ABC books are printed in bolder font and the words are longer. The students can also count the letters in the word, reinforcing that words are made of groups of letters. *F Is for Florida* (Farley & Mills, 2018) is particularly good for expanding children's vocabulary and making connections to things around their state.

Collaborative Writing

Alphabet books are perfect for using the collaborative writing strategy. This strategy is a way to introduce the writing process by creating a collaborative class book. After reading *F Is for Florida* (Farley & Mills, 2018), each student can write a page for the book. When writing collaborative books, the teacher should first model an example for the students and write the first page collaboratively (Tompkins, 2017).

When working with Emergent readers and writers, it is easier to use a template page so that students can complete it using familiar words. Some students may need scaffolding as they are only able to trace letters, add pictures, or copy words from word walls. After reading the ABC book about their state, students can make a book about their community or their school. Students can be provided the sentence stem "I see a _____" to add to their pictures. The teacher might choose to make a copy of the class book for each student or might place the specially bound original in the class library (Tompkins, 2017).

PICTURE BOOKS

Picture books tend to have brief texts written for learners from two through seven years of age. Picture books tend to average about 32 pages in length, including the cover pages, introduction, back flaps, and copyright information. Although the average is 32 pages, they can come in lengths that are multiples of eight. They rely on both text and illustrations to convey their meaning and can range from about 100 to 1,000 words. These books usually have one main character, one plot, and one story line. Picture books typically engage the reader through the use of rhyme, cadence, and repetition (Bowman, 2019). They often have remarkable illustrations that are truly works of art (Tompkins, 2017).

No, David! (Shannon, 1998) is a great picture book to use with Emergent readers for multiple reasons. Since its illustrations are drawn to mimic those of a young child, they help children believe they, too, are writers and illustrators. The content of the book provides an effective way to introduce students to the importance of following rules and making good classroom decisions.

Draw a Prediction

When Mrs. Aultman chose this story to read to her class, her instruction could have been made even more purposeful by using the reading strategy called draw a prediction. Making predictions is an essential strategy for reading. Students have to think ahead of the text and ask questions while reading. This process helps them to better understand the story, make connections as they read, and engage with the text (Lynch, 2021b).

To implement this strategy, Mrs. Aultman would strategically plan four stopping points as she reads, two for class discussion and two for drawing pictures. As she shows the cover of the book, she will ask the class, "What do you think Mama will say?" After posing the question, she will have the class discuss their predictions. For the second prediction, Mrs. Aultman will ask the students, "What do you think will happen when David reaches for the cookie jar?" At this stopping point, students are given time to draw their predictions. For the third stopping point, Mrs. Aultman will invite the students to consider the part of the story where David eats dinner, asking, "What do you think will happen at dinner?" The class will once again engage in a discussion. Finally, Mrs. Aultman will ask the class, "What do you think David will do in his room?" For this final prediction, students will engage in another drawing.

The story *No, David!* (Shannon, 1998) lends itself to discussing the characteristics of good citizens. It allows the teacher to discuss how students can be either peacemakers or peacebreakers based on their choices and provides the groundwork for the writing activity of constructing a list. Children can learn written language in the same manner they learn oral language. However, oral language differs in both form and function. Written language is a means to record events, important matters, or knowledge. While oral language can serve this same purpose, it is also used to communicate, socialize, and develop relationships (Literacy How, 2020).

T Chart Lists

Clay (2013) determined that reading and writing are reciprocal. However, the reciprocity is not automatic, which is why the role of the teacher is key. Teachers need to help students make these connections. One way teachers can support Emergent reading and writing is to have students make lists. Lists are authentic and serve a purpose. Children have most likely watched their parents make many lists. Lists are easy for children to organize, and students can write or draw about things that are relevant to them (Fried, 2006).

After reading *No, David!* (Shannon, 1998), the class can create a list or pictures of actions that identify peacemakers and peacebreakers. These lists can be constructed collaboratively on a T chart so students can see the comparison between the two types of behaviors. The list can then be posted as reference for conversations with students who may need to reflect on different choices or options for their actions, making this class-constructed list authentic and purposeful.

ANTICIPATION GUIDE REVISITED

At the start of this chapter, you considered four statements. After reading this chapter, reevaluate the anticipation guide statements and determine if your point of view has changed.

1. Children master oral language outside of the classroom setting; it can't be addressed in the classroom setting.
2. Key predictors of success for early literacy are alphabetic code, oral language, print concepts, and rhyming.
3. Phonological awareness and phonemic awareness are the same thing.

4. Telling stories with pictures is part of Emergent reading skills.

CONCLUSION

This chapter began with Mrs. Aultman reading *No, David!* (Shannon, 1998) to her Emergent readers. Consider some of the strategies that were used with the different types of texts and how these strategies could better link oral language and literacy for her Emergent readers and writers. Wordless picture books, predictable pattern books, nursery rhymes and rhyming books, ABC books, and fiction picture books are all types of authentic text that can be used to develop readers and writers. What happens in preschool and kindergarten classrooms matters, not only during a child's educational experiences but for their entire futures as well. When providing instruction for her Emergent readers and writers, Mrs. Aultman will intentionally integrate reading and writing activities to support her students' growth in both areas of literacy, making sure equal emphasis is placed on each of these skills.

STOP AND THINK

1. Think about each of the six types of connected, authentic texts reviewed in this chapter. Determine how these types of text are evident in your instruction for Emergent readers and writers. Complete table 2.1,

Table 2.1 Reading and Writing Activities across Genres

Genre	Text/Author	Reading Strategy	Writing Strategy
Wordless picture books			
Predictable pattern books			
Nursery rhymes			
Rhyming books			
ABC books			
Fiction picture books			

considering the scope and range of the reading and writing strategies used for each genre of text and how they can be implemented in your classroom. Do not include the same strategy more than once.
2. Based on the Emergent reading and writing strategies explained in this chapter, identify strategies you have learned about that you could use in your instruction. Describe how and when you would use each strategy and the reason for choosing the strategies for each type of authentic text.

REFERENCES

Achieve the Core. (n.d.). Foundations skills and practice strategies—kindergarten and first grade. Student Achievement Partners. https://achievethecore.org/content/upload/Foundational%20Skills%20Practice%20Strategies.pdf

Adolph, S. M., Catts, H. W., & Lee, J. (2010, May 12). Kindergarten predictors of second vs. eighth grade reading comprehension impairments. *Journal of Learning Disabilities*, *43*(4), 332–345.

Allyn, P., & Morrell, E. (2016). *Every child a super reader: 7 strengths to open a world of possible*. Scholastic.

Barone, Diane M. (2010). *Children's literature in the classroom: Engaging lifelong readers*. Guilford Publications.

Beech, J. R. (2005). Ehri's model of phases of learning to read: A brief critique. *Journal of Research in Reading*, *28*(1), 50–58.

Bennett, C. (2019, October 29). The importance of nursery rhymes in early childhood. World Nursery Rhyme Week. https://www.pacey.org.uk/news-and-views/pacey-blog/2019/october-2019/the-importance-of-nursery-rhymes-in-early-childhoo/

Blackwell-Bullock, R., Invernizzi, M., Drake, E. A., & Howell, J. L. (n.d.). Concept of Word in text: An integral literacy skill. Virginia State Reading Association.

Bolduc, J., & Lefebvre, P. (2012). Using nursery rhymes to foster phonological and musical processing skills in kindergarteners. *Creative Education*, *34*, 495–502.

Bowman, J. (2019, January 12). What genre is my children's book? https://www.jennybowman.com/what-genre-is-my-childrens-book/#:~:text=Picture%20Books&text=Though%20the%20standard%20is%2032,%E2%80%931000%20words%2C%20sometimes%20more

Burnett, C. (2018, April 16). Reading without words: The why and how of wordless books. Scholastic. https://www.scholastic.com/parents/books-and-reading/raise-a-reader-blog/reading-without-words-why-and-how-wordless-books.html

Clay. M. M. (2000). *Running records for classroom teachers*. Heinemann.

Clay, M. M. (2013). *An observation survey of early literacy achievement*. Mary Clay Literacy Trust.

Collins, K., & Glover, M. (2015). *I am reading: Nurturing young children's meaning making and joyful engagement with any book*. Heinemann.

Cunningham, P. (2013). *Phonics they use: Words for reading and writing* (3rd ed.). Pearson.

dePaola, T. (1978). *Pancakes for Breakfast*. Houghton Mifflin Harcourt.

Dewdney, A. (2005). *Llama llama red pajama*. Penguin Group.

Edelin-Smith, P. J (1997). How now brown cow: Phoneme awareness activities for collaborative classrooms. *Intervention in School and Clinic, 33*(2), 103–111.

Ehri, L. (1999). Phases of development in learning to read words. In J. Oakhill & R. Beard (Eds.), *Reading development and the teaching of reading: A psychological perspective* (pp. 79–108). Blackwell.

Ehri, L., Nunes, S. R., Willows, D. M., Schuster, B. V., Yaghoub-Zadeh, Z., & Shanahan, T. (2001). Phonemic awareness instruction helps children learn to read: Evidence from the National Reading Panel's meta-analysis. *Reading Research Quarterly, 36*(3), 250–287.

Farley, C., & Miles, S. (2018). *F is for Florida: Sunshine state ABC primer*. WorkmanPublishing.

Fried, M. D. (2006, Spring). Reciprocity: Promoting the flow of knowledge for learning to read and write. *Journal of Reading Recovery*, 5–14.

Giles, R. M., & Tunks, K. W. (2010). Children write their world: Environmental print as a teaching tool. *Dimensions of Early Childhood, 38*(3), 23–30.

Grofcikova, S., & Macajova, M. (2021). Rhyming in the context of the phonological awareness of pre-school children. *C•E•P•S Journal, 11*(1), 115–138. https://files.eric.ed.gov/fulltext/EJ1296910.pdf

Hamman, J. (2019, December 6). 8 research-backed ways to aid struggling emergent readers. Edutopia. George Lucas Educational Foundation. https://www.edutopia.org/article/8-research-backed-ways-aid-struggling-emergent-readers

Hart, B. M., & Risley, R. (1995). *Meaningful differences in the everyday experience of young American children*. Brookes Publishing.

Khalil, H. H. (2017, May). A pragmatic analysis of vague language in the news articles on the Iraqi security crisis. *Theory and Practice in Language Studies, 7*(5), 327–355.

Linder, R. (2014). *K–2 chart sense: Common sense charts to teacher K–2 informational text and literature*. The Literacy Initiative.

Lindfors, J. W. (2008). *Children's language: Connecting reading, writing, and talk*. Teachers College Press.

Literacy How. (2020). Oral language: What is it? https://www.literacyhow.org/oral-language/#:~:text=Oral%20language%20(OL)%2C%20sometimes,as%20a%20predictor%20for%20both

Lynch, M. (2020, November 24). Understanding letter recognition and its role in preliteracy. *The Edvocate*. https://www.theedadvocate.org/understanding-letter-recognition-and-its-role-in-preliteracy/

Lynch, M. (2021a, April 2). Why understanding onset and rime is essential to reading. *The Edvocate*. https://www.theedadvocate.org/why-understanding-onset-and-rime-is-essential-to-reading/

Lynch, M. (2021b, April 3). Using predictions to improve your students' reading comprehension skills. *The Edvocate.* https://www.theedadvocate.org/using-prediction-to-improve-your-students-reading-comprehension-skills/

Lyon, G. R. (1995). Toward a definition of dyslexia. *Annals of Dyslexia, 45,* 3–27.

Martin, B. (1967). *Brown bear, brown bear.* Henry Holt.

McGee, L. M., & Schickedanz, J. A. (2007). Repeated interactive read-alouds in preschool and kindergarten. *The Reading Teacher, 60*(8), 742–751.

Moats, L., & Tolman, C. (2009). The development of phonological skills. Reading Rockets. https://www.readingrockets.org/article/development-phonological-skills

National Center for Family Literacy. (2009). *Developing early literacy: Report of the National Early Literacy Panel.* National Institute for Literacy. https://lincs.ed.gov/publications/pdf/NELPSummary.pdf#xml=http://search.nifl.gov/texis/search/pdfhi.txt?query=Developing+Early+Literacy%3A+Report+of+the+National+Early+Literacy+Panel&pr=LINCS&prox=page&rorder=500&rprox=500&rdfreq=500&rwfreq=500&rlead=500&

National Reading Panel. (2000, April). *Teaching children to read: An evidence-based assessment of the scientific research literature on reading and its implications for reading instruction.* U.S. Government Printing Office.

Nikol, M. K. (2021). Sharing the pen: An exploration of interactive writing in early childhood classrooms. *Montana English Journal, 43*(1), 45–48.

Okello, B. (2021, January 28). The power of read alouds: How to perform an effective read aloud. University of Notre Dame Center for Literacy Education. https://iei.nd.edu/initiatives/notre-dame-center-for-literacy-education/news/the-power-of-read-alouds-how-to-perform

Reed, D. (2016, November 29). Comprehension skills are important for readers of all ages. Iowa Reading Research Center. https://iowareadingresearch.org/blog/comprehension-skills-are-important-for-readers-of-all-ages

Reutzal, R. (1985). Story maps improve comprehension. *Reading Teacher, 38,* 400–404.

Schickedanz, J. A., & Collins, M. F. (2013). *The early phases of reading and writing.* National Association for the Education of Young Children.

Serravallo, J. (2017). *The writing strategies book: Your everything guide to developing skilled writers.* Heinemann.

Shannon, D. (1998). *No, David!* The Blue Sky Press.

Slater, J. M. (2002). Nursery rhymes in a balanced literacy approach. Center on Disabilities Technology and Persons with Disabilities 2002 Conference Proceedings. http://www.csun.edu/~hfdss006/conf/2002/proceedings/32.htm

Smith S. B., Simmons, D. C., & Kame'enui, E. J. (1998). Phonological awareness: Instructional and curricular basics and implications. In D. C. Simmons & E. J. Kame'enui (Eds.), *What reading research tells us about children with diverse learning needs: Bases and basics.* Lawrence Erlbaum Associates.

Stewart, J. (2004). *Jack be nimble.* Continental Press.

Tankersley, K. (2003). *The threads of literacy: Strategies for literacy development.* ASCD.

Texas Education Agency. (2002). *Guidelines for examining phonics and word recognition programs.* Texas Reading Initiative.

Tompkins, G. E. (2017). *Literacy for the twenty-first century: A balanced approach* (7th ed.). Pearson.

Tunks, K. W., & Giles, R. M. (2007). *Write now! Publishing with young authors: PreK–grade 2*. Heinemann.

University of Oregon. (n.d.). Big ideas in beginning reading. Center on Teaching and Learning. http://reading.uoregon.edu/big_ideas/pa/pa_sequence.php

Victoria State Government. (2020, June). Concept of print. https://www.education.vic.gov.au/school/teachers/teachingresources/discipline/english/literacy/readingviewing/Pages/litfocusconceptsprint.aspx#:~:text=%E2%80%8BConcepts%20of%20Print%20refers,that%20print%20conveys%20a%20message

Warner, L., & Weiss, S. (2005). Why young children need alphabet books. *Kappa Delta Pi, 43*, 124–127.

Whorrall, J., & Cabell, S. (2015, June 17). Supporting children's oral language development in the preschool classroom. *Early Childhood Education Journal,* (44), 335–331. https://web.s.ebscohost.com/ehost/pdfviewer/pdfviewer?vid=0&sid=45e7557d-bbf8–40aa-9683-addc9b7cbdde%40redis

Chapter 3

Beginning Stage

Cheri Gallman and Lin Carver

Walking into her room one morning, Mrs. Townsend, a first-grade teacher, was full of excitement as she looked at her eager class of Beginning readers. That day, as she had done many mornings before, she had her morning message on her board centered in the front of the room. She had written the message in large manuscript letters so it would be easy for everyone to read. In the message, she reminded the students of what they were learning that week (see figure 3.1).

Often she began the morning message with "Good morning, Class." Most of the students were able to read that phrase no matter where she placed it. She noticed that only 4 of her 21 students were still struggling to read the

> Good morning, Class. Today is Tuesday, March 7, 2022. Do you remember what it means to infer? Today we will see what we can infer from our book, Puppy Trouble. Do you think he will go in the car? Have a great day!

Figure 3.1 Morning Message

word "morning" with her. The rest of them seem to be starting to build a sight vocabulary, she thought excitedly.

Today is going to be different, she thought to herself. All the students should be able to read this message. Today's morning message was almost the same as those on the last two days. The only new word should be the word "infer."

At the beginning of class, she pointed to each word in the message as the class read the message out loud together. She noticed that some of the students only read the last line, "Have a great day!," which had been the same for the last three weeks. Mrs. Townsend noticed that her students' performance was inconsistent. Sometimes they seemed to know a word, while at other times they had no idea what it said. She wondered, "Is this the way it happens for all first-grade teachers? Shouldn't all my students be able to read the message by now? After all, they are at the Beginning reading stage." She worried that maybe she was just going about the whole teaching reading and writing thing wrong.

ANTICIPATION GUIDE

Read the following four statements before reading the chapter. Decide if you agree or disagree with each statement. Then read the chapter. After reading the chapter, revisit the anticipation guide and decide if your views are the same or have changed.

1. Concept of Word develops along a continuum.
2. The terms "sight words" and "high-frequency" words can be used interchangeably.
3. Leveled readers and decodable texts represent the same theoretical philosophy of Beginning reading.
4. Systematic, sequential phonics instruction should be provided for all learners.

CHARACTERISTICS OF BEGINNING READERS

The stage that follows Emergent reading and writing is the Beginning reader and writer stage. During this stage, which might have different names depending on who you read, students are developing reading and writing behaviors based on their developing understanding of the alphabetic principle (Gehsmann & Templeton, 2022). Because of this developing alphabetic skill, this stage is sometimes referred to as the partial-alphabetic stage (Ehri,

1999). During this stage, students can recognize some letters of the alphabet and begin to combine this information with the context to build a sight vocabulary, as Mrs. Townsend's students were doing with the morning message. Learners in this stage begin by finger pointing predictable memorized texts and during this stage move to less familiar texts. They are developing the Concept of Word, but may at times experience difficulty identifying individual words in context.

Concept of Word

Concept of Word in context is a valid and reliable predictor of first-grade reading achievement (Warley et al., 2005). Often Concept of Word has focused just on the match between speech and print and the student's ability to point to a word on the page. However, this concept actually involves the automatic knowledge of letter sounds, the ability to isolate beginning consonant sounds, and the ability to remember words in isolation (Flanigan, 2007). Consequently, Concept of Word is not a single skill; it occurs along a developmental continuum (Blackwell-Bulllock et al., n.d.). By the middle of this stage, most children have developed a full Concept of Word and can read many words both in and out of context. During the middle of this stage, learners are beginning to focus more intentionally on building a sight vocabulary through automatic word recognition (Gehsmann & Templeton, 2022).

As students are developing this skill, it is evidenced in their ability to process a sentence like the following: "See the red mat." Students who have developed Concept of Word will be able to recognize that there are four words in the sentence. They will be able to count and point to the individual words as they are being read to them and understand that each printed word corresponds to a spoken word. Once students have mastered the Concept of Word, they are ready to identify the phonemes within the word.

Sight Words and High-Frequency Words

Sight words are those words that children can read automatically or by "sight" in about a quarter of a second (Raynor et al., 2001). During the Beginning stage of reading, learners typically master a bank of about 150 sight words. Not all students will have the same words in their sight word bank because learners master more easily the words to which they ascribe significance. Sight words are often confused with high-frequency words. Sight words are a subset of high-frequency words that may not be easily decodable since they do not always follow the standard phonetic patterns (Mulvahill, 2022). These high-frequency words can be found on the Fry Instant Word List or the Dolch list, both of which can be easily accessed online. The Fry Instant Word List

(Fry & Kress, 2006) is based on an expansion of the Dolch list, which was originally constructed in 1936.

Often sight words and high-frequency words are taught by rote memorization because some of them do not follow English pronunciation rules. However, findings based on the Science of Reading suggest that we expand strategies beyond just rote memorization. Some high-frequency words are so irregular that they are learned more easily as whole units, but high-frequency words occur along a continuum from irregular to phonetically predictable (Miles et al., 2019). Most high-frequency words are at least decodable in part (Gehsmann & Templeton, 2022). For those more phonemically regular words, phoneme-grapheme mapping can be used, in which students first map out the sounds they hear in the word, then add the graphemes that match those sounds. Teaching students to decode in this way by connecting letter-sound correspondences to the spellings of high-frequency words will help them to retain the information (Ehri, 2014). In addition, beginning exposure to the word within a text can make instruction more meaningful and memorable as students learn to map the phonemes to the graphemes (Gehsmann & Templeton, 2022). Readers are progressing from reading these words in isolation to automatically identifying them in context. Students may practice identifying these words in context using reading strategies, such as cross-checking or predicting (Ministry of Education, 2016).

Phonics Skills

During the Emergent stage learners developed phonemic awareness skills, and now in the Beginning stage they are progressing to developing phonics skills through matching individual phonemes to their graphemes. Children at the Beginning reading stage learn the relationships between letters and sounds and printed and spoken words. As these phoneme-grapheme correspondence skills are improving, learners begin to rely on phonics skills to decode words (Tompkins, 2017).

Children at this stage should be taught phonics rules to help them begin decoding and recognizing words. By the end of this stage they have acquired a general understanding of the spelling-sound system. Direct teaching of decoding helps to promote development. The Simple View of Reading tells us that decoding plays a crucial role in reading comprehension (Gough & Tunmer, 1986).

The primary focus of phonics instruction is to help Beginning readers to understand how letters and sounds are linked for reading and spelling. Systematic phonics instruction builds on a foundation of well-developed phonemic awareness skills, which provides significant benefits for Beginning readers (National Reading Panel, 2000).

Children are using words in their speech and Beginning reading that contain morphemes, but they rarely think about the morphemes contained in each word. Through early morphological analysis, learners begin to understand the function of the inflectional suffixes and how these are used in multiple settings. During the Beginning reading and writing stage, students are exposed to suffixes such as "-ed," "-ing," "-s," "-er," and "-ful."

Language and Vocabulary Development

Often when teachers discuss vocabulary, they refer to the words students need to learn in order to comprehend a written text. But actually, "vocabulary" is a more encompassing term. It refers to both expressive and receptive vocabulary. These two types of vocabulary can be further divided into four main types. The two expressive types of vocabulary are speaking and writing, while the two receptive types are listening and reading. Vocabulary refers both to the list of words and the range of words known by an individual. A person's vocabulary develops with age, experience, and learning (Wollacott, 2022).

The emphasis during instruction for Beginning readers tends to be on developing automaticity and accuracy in reading and writing of sight and high-frequency words. However, language and vocabulary instruction cannot be overlooked. Early experiences with language can have significant impact on later reading achievement (Hruby, 2020). An interesting fact is that as children mature, changes in their brains after about the ages of nine or ten make learning vocabulary more difficult (Hruby, 2020). Providing learners with extensive language experiences impacts knowledge and intellectual ability, which affect their comprehension of texts. Through exposure to various genres, children move from the informal oral language structures to the more formal discourse of written English, resulting in exposure to much more general academic vocabulary as well as content- or domain-specific academic language (Gehsmann & Templeton, 2022).

Academic vocabulary refers to the language used in educational settings. Academic vocabulary helps students to communicate and think about specific subject area information and is needed to express abstract and technical ideas that do not tend to occur in social or casual conversation (Sedita, 2016). Read alouds can expose learners to general academic terms such as "opposite," "combination," and "infer," which can result in an increase in the quantity and quality of students' vocabulary.

During exposure to thematic units and informational picture books, students are continuing to learn about the world around them. These activities help students learn about content- or domain-specific vocabulary. Through teachers sharing "kid friendly" definitions (Beck et al., 2013) and discussing vocabulary presented in context, it is easy to extend children's vocabulary through the use of why questions. Asking why leads to deeper thinking about words and increases students' opportunities to improve their vocabulary, intellectual ability, and subject area knowledge (Gehsmann & Templeton, 2022).

As was evident in Mrs. Townsend's morning message, the message provides an opportunity to build vocabulary. The content was built on the academic instruction in previous settings, so the background knowledge would have been developed by discussing the same topics and reviewing vocabulary. Background knowledge plays a very important role in comprehension. The cognitive strategy of activating prior knowledge has two parts, mobilizing knowledge and searching existing schemata (Olson, 2011). Background knowledge can be thought of as a bridge between the reader and the text. Without background knowledge, students may find a text too difficult, may lose motivation, and may possibly give up on reading (Tompkins, 2017). Furthermore, background knowledge is an important component of inferring, which is the skill on which Mrs. Townsend's class was working. When inferencing, students tap into their background knowledge, use evidence from the text, and then create an inference (Tompkins, 2017).

READING CONNECTED TEXT

During the Beginning stage, children start to read stories containing high-frequency and phonically regular words, and they use emerging decoding skills to "sound out" new one-syllable words. A major difference in this stage from the Emergent stage is that these readers do not rely as significantly on the pictures within the text. Beginning readers use the cueing systems to apply multiple strategies to predict words and meaning. They use both pictorial and language cues.

However, they are shifting their information-gathering emphasis from the picture to the words in the text. But pictures are still an important textual feature. The pictures provide a way to supplement background knowledge and further develop the story concepts. They act as cues for identifying more difficult words or concepts and for illustrating the meaning within specific contexts while increasing engagement. Pictures can also help to develop an understanding of the meaning of the text (Newton, 2006).

These Beginning readers are developing awareness of the role of punctuation, locating high-frequency words, using directionality correctly, and even starting to answer some discussion questions. In this stage, students are able to use one-to-one correspondence to distinguish between words in a sentence, use fewer picture clues, identify sight words, and use punctuation. Students at this level are starting to self-correct and to talk about the text. Strategies such as self-monitoring help develop important metacognitive skills. "The priority people place on various cueing systems can vary; however, the phonological system is especially important for Beginning readers and writers as they apply phonics skills to decode and spell words" (Tompkins, 2014, p. 13).

CHARACTERISTICS OF TEXTS FOR BEGINNING READERS

At the beginning of this stage, students are frequently exposed to books through interactive read alouds. The teacher may choose to initiate these shared readings through the use of big books so that children can easily follow along as the teacher points to the words in the text (Parkes, 2000). As students develop more familiarity with texts, they expand the number of books they can read independently. These books may take the form of predictable books with repetition, cumulative sequences, rhyme and rhythm, and sequential patterns (Tompkins, 2017).

The category of early reader books is a rapidly expanding genre. They bridge the gap between picture books and chapter books. The use of early reader books can help to build confidence and independence. Choosing effective books to use with Beginning readers is very important. There are numerous factors to consider. First is the physical appearance of the book; the layout should support early independence. The font of the text should be large and easy to read, and it should be clear and consistent throughout the book. A clear contrast between the words and the pictures is particularly important at this stage. Dark illustrations should be paired with white text, while dark text is easier to read on white pages. Pictorial support should be spread throughout the text, and the illustrations should be chosen to help the reader understand the setting, characters, and emotions. These illustrations can provide context clues for enhancing comprehension. The story should be organized into short sections, paragraphs, or chapters, with use of white space between lines, paragraphs, and chapters (Buikema, 2020).

Another important consideration is the content. The story should be built around a particular character or genre. It is important that the reader find the characters in the text lovable and relatable. Once students find lovable and relatable characters, they will be motivated to read additional books by that same author. For Beginning readers, texts should be short stories that begin as predictable texts but build to increased complexity.

The next important consideration is the vocabulary used within the book. It is important for teachers to choose books that introduce new words but also include repeated phrases, sentence structures, and rhyming to reinforce language development and phonemic awareness (Trevino, 2015).

CHARACTERISTICS OF BEGINNING WRITERS

Just as reading develops through stages, so does writing. During the Beginning stage, learners develop in their ability to use phonics to decode and spell words. During this stage, they can print all of the upper- and lower-case letters and create basic sentences that begin with capital letters and end with punctuation. They are learning that writing goes from left to right, with spaces between words. As they are learning to read about 50 high-frequency and sight words, they are learning to spell them as well. Simple stories are developing a simple beginning, middle, and end, and children are able to read their writing to their classmates (Tompkins, 2017).

These learners can use their knowledge to segment and blend most one-syllable words, so they are able to spell many three- and four-letter short vowel words correctly, but they will use inventive spelling when necessary. Toward the end of the Beginning reader and writer stage, students begin to use portions of the writing process such as planning, drafting, rereading for meaning, and self-correction. Writers are beginning to create brief stories, descriptions, and journal entries (Snow et al., 1998).

INSTRUCTIONAL METHODS

There are a variety of scientifically based authentic reading and writing strategies that teachers can incorporate in their lessons for Beginning readers. It is important to note that high-quality instruction consists of core literacy skills that target multiple areas such as phonemic awareness and phonics instruction that address word, syllable, and phonemic levels (MacLeod-Vidal & Smith, 2021). When implementing these strategies, teachers should incorporate a multisensory approach that emphasizes visual, auditory, and kinesthetic-tactile modalities in order to reach all students (Schukraft, 2020). Oral language facilitates writing development and vice versa, which is evidenced in the relationship among oral language, written language, and reading. The connection between the expressive and receptive systems is crucial for the child's literacy development (Lindfors, 2008).

There are numerous science-based reading and writing strategies that teachers can employ in their classrooms to advance their students' literacy skills. This chapter examines five examples of reading and writing strategies that can be used with Beginning readers across different genres.

Gradual Release

The gradual release model is a four-step process that promotes active learning and retention. This process involves describing a strategy explicitly, modeling the strategy in action, providing opportunities for guided practice, and then allowing students to use the strategy independently. Combined, all of the steps of the gradual release model are critical for helping readers achieve mastery (Zemelman et al., 2012). Teaching students to transfer and apply strategies will help to give them access to increasingly complex texts to encourage higher order and critical thinking as they continue to grow as learners.

USING TEXTS WITH BEGINNING READERS

Possible texts are everywhere in the Beginning readers' and writers' classroom! They are on the walls, in textbooks, in classroom libraries, on the board, and on digital devices. These all provide authentic text that can be used in instruction. In this chapter we focus on illustrating methods for integrating reading and writing instruction using real connected texts from five genres typically found in the Beginning readers' and writers' classroom.

Kilpatrick (2015) identified three essential components for reading instruction: instruction in phonemic awareness skills to an advanced automatic level; explicit, systematic phonics instruction; and opportunities for authentic reading of real, connected texts. "Connected texts" refers to text containing multiple sentences on a single page or over related pages that tell a story or present cohesive information. Connected text can be found in teacher-created information such as the morning message, decodable books such as *Barb and Her Car* (Knight, n.d.), leveled readers such as *Kitty Cat and the Bird* (Smith, n.d.), informational picture books such as *National Geographic Kids: Spiders* (Marsh, 2011), and Beginning reader series such as *Mary Lou Melon* (Lovell, 2001).

TEACHER CREATED

During the morning message, Mrs. Townsend was using a daily literacy routine with her students in which the teacher and the students read the text orally together (Tompkins, 2017). In this routine, before the students arrive the teacher writes a brief message about what will happen that day. There are a number of versions of this activity.

Fill-in-the-Blank Message

Perhaps Mrs. Townsend would have experienced even more success had she incorporated before-reading strategies to help build background knowledge and increase confidence. Before reading the message, the class may have discussed the calendar and what they learned the day before. Another option would have been that rather than just having the students read the message together, Mrs. Townsend could have covered some of the words in the morning message and asked the class to help her determine which word would make sense in the sentence. This type of activity would have provided an opportunity to build vocabulary, syntax, and comprehension skills.

Elkonin Boxes

In our morning message, Mrs. Townsend could have covered up the word "car" with a sticky note. She chose this word because the class was studying how to decode words with "-ar" blends. To further support the acquisition of this skill, each child would be given a page with Elkonin boxes and a set of round tabs (see figure 3.2). As Mrs. Townsend says the word orally, students push one marker into each box to represent the sounds they hear in the word.

Word Ladders

Another activity Mrs. Townsend might consider using during her morning message time to further involve her students would be to encourage children to circle any words in the message that contain the r-controlled vowel sounds for /ar/. In this message there are two words, "March" and "car." After the students read the morning message, the teacher could also have had them practice the "-ar" combination by reading "-ar" word ladders (Tompkins, 2017). These ladders present a list of individual words with the letters organized as steps on a ladder. For each of the words the "-ar" is in the medial position,

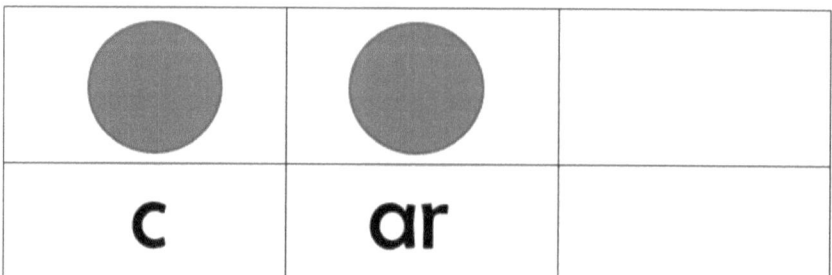

Figure 3.2 Elkonin Boxes

but each contains different initial and final consonant sounds. Today's word ladder list could have five words: "barn," "mark," "cart," "part," and "park."

Tomorrow Mrs. Townsend hopes to use a more interactive morning message. Adding an interactive component tends to increase student motivation and engagement and builds classroom community (Walton, 2020). In the interactive message, Mrs. Townsend will use a Fill-in-the Blank morning message focusing on the /ar/ sound that relates to the phonics minilesson the class will be working on about words containing the /ar/ sound (see figure 3.3).

The first thing she will do is to have the class read the message together, inserting the words they think make sense in each blank. Then Mrs. Townsend will place sticky notes at the bottom of the message. She will have written one word on each sticky note. The notes will contain the words "cars," "Barb," "car, "start," and "park." The class will then work together to place one of the notes in each blank in the story. This strategy helps students practice the decoding skills they are learning while using their developing self-monitoring strategies to understand the meaning and visual cues from the text.

Interactive Writing

A shared or interactive writing activity after the lesson on *Barb and Her Car* (Knight, n.d.) can be used to effectively integrate reading and writing. During interactive writing, the class members and the teacher work together to create the message. Students can collaborate on ideas about places Barb likes to drive her car as the teacher acts as a scribe, demonstrating correct spacing between words, spelling, and punctuation. This new written text can be displayed in the classroom as a model for students to reference as needed.

Happy Wednesday, Class.

Today we will read more about _____.

We will read a book called _____ and her _____. She loves to _____ her car and drive to the _____.

Figure 3.3 Fill-in-the-Blank Morning Message

DECODABLE TEXTS

Decodable texts are used to support phonics instruction in the Science of Reading (Southard, 2022). These decodable texts are books that students can decode once they have been explicitly taught the letter to sound relationships covered in the specific text. Often the terms "decodable texts" and "leveled readers" are used interchangeably. Decodable readers focus on the "code" and contain a large number of phonetically regular words that can be sounded out once a student has the phonetic knowledge. In order to solidify foundational skills, teachers must provide students with opportunities to capitalize on orthographic learning in decodable texts based on phonemic awareness processes and phonics (Burkins & Yates, 2021). Teachers need to select decodable readers that emphasize the sound-symbol relationships their students are learning. It is important for teachers to remember that the letter-sound relationships must be explicitly taught before they expect students to use the skill in connected text.

When using a decodable text, students need to begin by identifying the sound-symbol relationship so that they can blend the sounds to read the words from the text. Students need to understand that the sounds they are learning can be transferred to reading connected texts. Many decodable books will have the words included in the book listed on the inside cover. When students sound out the word, encourage them to read the word again but as a whole word to reinforce automaticity.

Repeated Readings

Repeated readings are an effective way to increase automaticity and comprehension. Repeated reading has been used for many years and is based on the ideas proposed by Samuels (1979) and later embraced by the National Reading Panel (2000). Readers need to be able to decode without thinking so that they can devote cognitive space to understanding the text. Shanahan (2015) built on these ideas by recommending using short 50- to 200-word texts that are at the reader's frustration level and limiting repeated readings to three times.

A Bed for Bug is a decodable text that focuses on the skill of decoding words containing the short vowel sound. The short "e" sound is the new sound introduced in this text. This book can be introduced through a picture walk. A picture walk is a shared activity between the teacher and the children before reading an unfamiliar story. During the picture walk, the pictures in the story help to familiarize the reader with the story prior to introducing the text (Hands and Voices, 2014). In this story the picture walk would be used to expand science concepts as students discuss the meaning of the words "bugs" and "insects," the body parts illustrated in the bug, and the comparison of the types of bugs.

Echo Reading

Echo reading could be used with this text. Echo reading is a rereading strategy designed to help students develop expression, fluency, and print knowledge. The teacher reads a short segment of text, sometimes a sentence or short paragraph, and the students echo it back (Jennings et al., 2014). It is important that in this strategy the teacher makes sure to point to the words when reading so students can gain the letter to print concept.

Twister Spell and Read

Since this book focuses on the short vowel sounds, Twister Spell and Read is an effective way to practice blending consonants and short vowels into words. To create this game, the teacher covers each colored space on a Twister game mat with a different single consonant, a few consonant blends, or a short vowel. The teacher should create a list of short vowel words that can be made from the letters on the board. The teacher or another student reads a word from the list, and the students spell the word by covering the letters with their hands and feet. If the students answer correctly, they get another turn. If the answer is wrong, the students are out and go back to their seats, where they write that word on a sheet of paper and draw a picture to go with it. Play can continue until all the words are found or until everyone has a turn (Frugal Fun for Boys and Girls, 2022).

Leveled Readers

Leveled readers are written with instruction in mind. Typically, they have controlled vocabulary, limited sentence length, and often repetitive sentence structure (Weakland, 2020). Leveled readers focus on meaning and repeatedly use high-frequency words such as "said," "where," and "out," and syntactic patterns (Murray et al., 2014). There are many systems for leveling text such as Lexiles, Accelerated Reader, and Fountas and Pinnell, to name a few. Reading A–Z is another program of leveled readers. This program has 29 different levels of readers in its series (Learning A–Z, 2022).

These books include the use of many high-frequency words. In these texts, words are often not decodable based on the phonics instruction children have received. These texts may require the child to guess an unknown word based on a predictable pattern, picture clues, or context. This method might encourage readers to guess words using the three cueing systems—syntactic, graphophonic, and semantic systems—and not focus on the brain's ability to map these words into long-term memory (Five for Five, 2021).

One advantage of leveled texts is that they were created using natural speech patterns that can lift the level of students' oral language. Improving a student's oral language helps the reader to read more fluently and increases overall comprehension (LiteracyPages, 2018). Leveled readers instead of decodable texts are often included as part of a balanced literacy program rather than one based on the Science of Reading.

Leader and Chorus Choral Reading

A Day for Dad (Curran, n.d.) is a realistic fiction text of 67 words that is classified as a Level D leveled reader. It is intended for first-grade students as they talk about Father's Day. Each page begins with "Dad and I" and ends with the phrase "on Father's Day." The structure of the sentences in this book is perfect for a version of leader and chorus choral reading (Tompkins, 2017). The entire group reads the repeating parts of the pages while the teacher or a designated child reads the new section on each page.

Class Book

After reading the text, writing is integrated through the creation of a class book "On Father's Day." Each student is given a sheet of paper and some crayons. The students each draw a picture of an activity they like to do with Dad or another male member of their family. Then they write a sentence about their picture. The picture pages are then combined to form a class book, which is placed in the classroom library. Students can enjoy their class book during independent reading.

NONFICTION-INFORMATIONAL TEXT

National Geographic for Kids has many informational texts available. Even though there may be many words students are not ready to read independently, these informational texts are particularly appealing to this age group because these readers are typically interested in learning about their world (Shanahan, 2015). These texts can be used during independent reading or during instructional time as part of a thematic content area unit.

KWL

For the text *Spiders!* (Marsh, 2011), teachers can activate background knowledge by having students create a KWL chart about spiders and insects before reading. KWL charts can be used throughout reading instruction, before, during, and after the lesson. Used before instruction, they can activate prior knowledge. During the lesson, they can help students become active learners. Used after the lesson, this strategy can help to promote analysis, organization, and ownership of learning.

Cross-Grade Reading Buddies

Cross-grade reading buddies, in which students read or reread a selection with a classmate or an older student, is a strategy that can be used effectively with informational texts (Tompkins, 2017). In addition to building literacy skills, the conversations that occur between buddies can help to develop academic language skills. Reading the informational text to their buddies provides learners a fun way to practice oral reading skills for an authentic audience. During this activity, the older buddy can provide support by using a checklist to visually illustrate their buddy's progress. The Beginning readers can also work on comprehension skills by going back and checking their KWL chart with their buddies.

Writing is integrated into this activity as students complete their KWL throughout the reading process. Students can also work with their buddies to complete a Venn diagram that compares and contrasts spiders and insects. When these are completed, students can present their information to the whole group.

Sketch to Stretch

A sketch to stretch activity can be used to integrate writing. It is a tool for helping students expand their comprehension of the content they have read. Students individually or in small groups draw pictures or diagrams to represent the important concepts from the text (Beers, 2003). Students can discuss their illustrations and label their pictures to capture the most important concepts (Tompkins, 2017).

BEGINNING READER FICTION SERIES

The Molly Lou Melon Series, a three-book series by Lovell (2001), is an example of fiction texts that can be used to teach literacy skills through an interactive read aloud while also supporting students' social emotional learning by encouraging students to be proud no matter who they are and no matter what anybody else thinks or says. The teacher should introduce the book using a before-reading strategy of having students make connections to the content by identifying things that make them unique or different. Then the class can discuss whether being different is bad or not.

Think Aloud

As teachers are preparing for the read aloud, they should decide on stopping points throughout the book based on students' needs and skills. Teachers are then ready to begin the interactive read aloud. During an interactive read aloud, the book may be read more than one time. Teachers should have several comprehension questions ready to use in the during-reading phase (Bessick, 2022). During the reading, involve the students in a think aloud. During a think aloud, the teacher or the students say out loud what they are thinking about when reading. By verbalizing their inner speech, teachers can model how expert thinkers solve a problem. This lets students know that they are not alone in having to think their way through the problem-solving process. This process is often used to model comprehension processes such as making predictions, connecting with prior knowledge, monitoring comprehension, and word identification (Teacher Vision Staff, 2019).

Stop and Jot

Stop and jot is a writing strategy that works well with this type of a text. Teachers should determine a point in the story where they want to stop. It is important to first model the stop and jot strategy for students. Then, following the gradual release process, the class works together to complete one. During the third stopping place in the story, allow the students to independently stop and jot. Students can use their stop and jot notes to create an interactive journal entry. To support the story, students can draw in their journals something that is different about them. Students can label the pictures with a phrase or a complete sentence depending on where they are in the Beginning stage of reading and writing. Students who are further along in this stage might want to write advice to help Molly Lou Melon. Technology can be incorporated by having students record their thinking or response on an asynchronous social media program like Flipgrid (Powers, 2021).

ANTICIPATION GUIDE REVISITED

At the beginning of the chapter, you examined four statements. Based upon what you have read in this chapter, revisit the anticipation guide statements and decide if your views are the same or have changed.

1. Concept of Word develops along a continuum.
2. The terms "sight words" and "high-frequency words" can be used interchangeably.
3. Leveled readers and decodable texts represent the same theoretical philosophy of Beginning reading.
4. Systematic, sequential phonics instruction should be provided for all learners.

CONCLUSION

We began this chapter observing Mrs. Townsend as she worked with her group of Beginning readers and writers during the morning message. Using some of the strategies in this chapter, she could further support her learners through the various types of authentic texts found in the first-grade classroom: teacher created, decodable texts, leveled texts, Beginning reader series, and informational text. Throughout her instruction, Mrs. Townsend will be integrating reading and writing activities to support the synchronous development of both skills. Neither one occurs in a vacuum; one supports the other. During the year, students will practice these skills and continue to progress as they move through the stages of reading and writing development.

STOP AND THINK

1. Choose one of the genres of texts described in this chapter. Identify a specific text that would be appropriate for Beginning readers. Describe the Beginning reader text characteristics (qualitative, quantitative, and reader and text) that are evident that make this an appropriate choice for this level. Identify before-, during-, and after-reading strategies, and a writing strategy to use with this text.
2. Based on the strategies described in this chapter, identify additional strategies you have discovered that you could use in your instruction for Beginning readers and writers. Explain how and when you would use them.

3. How might digital resources be used to enhance print texts to better prepare our twenty-first-century learners?

REFERENCES

Beck, I. L., McKeown, J. G., & Kucan, L. (2013). *Bringing words to life: Robust vocabulary instruction* (2nd ed.). Gilford.

Beers, K. (2003). *When kids can't read what teachers can do: A guide for teachers 6–12*. Heinemann.

Bessick, P. (2022). How to plan an interactive read aloud in 5 easy steps. https://paigebessick.com/2017/02/how-to-plan-interactive-read-aloud-in-5.html

Blackwell-Bullock, R., Invernizzi, M., Drake, E., & Howell, J. (n.d.). Concept of word in text: An integral literacy skill. Reading Rockets. https://www.readingrockets.org/sites/default/files/concept-of-word.pdf

Buikema, E. (2020, March 27). White space in writing. *Writers in the Storm.* https://writersinthestormblog.com/2020/03/white-space-in-writing/#:~:text=White%20space%20draws%20the%20reader's,off%20reading%20quick%20and%20easy

Burkins, J., & Yates, K. (2021). *Shifting the balance: 6 ways to bring the Science of Reading into the balanced literacy classroom K–2*. Stenhouse.

Curran, A. (n.d.) *A day for dad*. A-Z Leveled Reader. https://www.readinga-z.com/book.php?id=1820

Ehri, L. (1999). Phases of development in learning to read words. In J. Oakhill & R. Beard (Eds.), *Reading development and the teaching of reading: A psychological perspective* (pp. 79–108). Blackwell.

Ehri, L. (2014). Orthographic mapping in the acquisition of sight word reading, spelling memory, and vocabulary learning. *Scientific Studies of Reading, 18*(1), 5–21.

Five for Five. (2021, May 26). Decodable books vs. leveled readers: Which type of books should beginning readers use? Pathways to Reading. https://pathwaystoreadinghomeschool.com/decodable-books-vs-leveled-readers/#:~:text=Words%20in%20a%20good%20decodable,to%20determine%20the%20unfamiliar%20words

Flanigan, K. (2007). A concept of word in text: A pivotal event in early reading acquisition. *Journal of Literacy Research, 39*(1), 37–70.

Frugal Fun for Boys and Girls. (2022). Twist and spell. https://frugalfun4boys.com/hands-on-activities-beginning-readers/

Fry, E. B., & Kress, J. E. (2006). *The reading teacher's book of lists: Grades K–12* (5th ed.). Jossey-Bass.

Gehsmann, K., & Templeton, S. (2022). *Teaching reading and writing: The developmental approach*. Pearson.

Gough, P. B., & Tunmer, W. E. (1986). Decoding, reading, and reading disability. *Remedial and Special Education, 7*, 6–10.

Hands And Voices. (2014). Taking a picture walk. https://www.handsandvoices.org/articles/education/ed/V11-2_picturewalk.htm

Hruby, G. (2020). Language's vanishing act in early literacy. *Phi Delta Kappan, 10*(5), 19–24.

Jennings, J., Caldwell, J., & Lerner, J. (2014). Reading problems assessment and teaching strategies. Pearson Education.

Kilpatrick, D. (2015). *The essentials of assessing, preventing, and overcoming reading difficulties*. Wiley.

Knight, K. (n.d.). *Barb and her car.* Reading A–Z. https://www.raz-plus.com/book.php?id=4217

Learning A–Z. (2022). Printable and projectable reading resources for K–5. https://www.learninga-z.com/site/products/readinga-z/overview?utm_source=google&utm_medium=cpc&utm_campaign={{campaign.name}}&utm_content={{adgroup.name}}&source=google&medium=cpc&campaign_id=17308981172&creative=599015211550&keyword=leveled%20readers&matchtype=p&network=g&device=c&gclid=CjwKCAjw2f-VBhAsEiwAO4lNeC4r5IQnil07ZCwwisHg2k3n7954ipNAZmxG18b_JJ2sF-Zg7q4wRhoCi7oQAvD_BwE

LiteracyPages. (2018, April 24). Leveled texts: A powerful instructional tool. Literacy in the Classroom. https://literacypages.wordpress.com/2018/04/24/the-benefits-of-using-leveled-texts/

Lovell, P. (2001). *Mary Lou Melon*. Putnam.

MacLeod-Vidal, H., & Smith, K. (2021). *Teach reading with Orton Gillingham*. Ulysses.

Marsh, L. (2011). *National Geographic readers: Spiders*. National Geographic Society.

Miles, K. P., McFadden, D. E., & Ehri, L. C. (2019). Associations between language and literacy skills and sight word learning for native and nonnative English-speaking kindergarteners. *Reading and Writing, 32*, 1681–1704.

Ministry of Education. (2016, March 22). Text processing strategies. Literacy Online. https://literacyonline.tki.org.nz/Literacy-Online/Planning-for-my-students-needs/Effective-Literacy-Practice-Years-5–8/Text-processing-strategies

Mulvahill, E. (2022, May 9). What are sight words? We Are Teachers. https://www.weareteachers.com/what-are-sight-words/

Murray, M., Munger, K., & Hiebert, E. (2014). An analysis of two reading intervention programs: How do the words, texts and programs compare? *The Elementary School Journal, 114*(4), 479–500.

National Reading Panel. (2000, April). *Teaching children to read: An evidence-based assessment of the scientific research literature on reading and its implications for reading instruction*. U.S. Government Printing Office.

Newton, D. P. (2006, July 6). The role of pictures in learning to read. *Educational Studies, 21*(1), 119–130. https://doi.org/10.1080/0305569950210109

Olson, C. B. (2011). *The reading/writing connection: Strategies for teaching and learning in the secondary classroom* (3rd ed.). Pearson.

Parkes, B. (2000). *Read it again! Revisiting shared reading*. Stenhouse.

Powers, M. (2021, March). Flipgrid. https://www.commonsense.org/education/website/flipgrid

Rayner, K., Foorman, B., Perfeti, C., Pesetsky, D., & Seidenberg, M. (2002, March 1). How should reading be taught? *Scientific American*, 85–91. https://www.scientificamerican.com/article/how-should-reading-be-tau/

Raynor, K., Foorman, B. R., Perfetti, C. A., Pesetsky, D., & Seidenberg, M. S. (2001). How psychological science informs the teaching of reading. *Psychological Science in the Public Interest, 2,* 31–73.

Samuels, S. J. (1979). The method of repeated readings. *The Reading Teacher, 32,* 403–408.

Schukraft, S. (2020, August 20). Multi-sensory learning: Types of instruction and materials. Institute for Multi-sensory Education. https://journal.imse.com/multi-sensory-learning-types-of-instruction-and-materials/

Sedita, J. (2016, March 8). Academic vocabulary. Keys to Literacy. https://keystoliteracy.com/blog/academic-vocabulary/

Shanahan, T. (2015, March 16). Informational text and young children. *Shanahan on Literacy*. Reading Rockets. https://www.readingrockets.org/blogs/shanahan-on-literacy/informational-text-and-young-children

Smith, A. (n.d.). *Kitty cat and the bird*. Rigby PM Stars.

Snow, C. E., Burns, M. S., & Griffin, P. (1998). *Preventing reading difficulties in young children*. National Academies Press. https://doi.org/10.17226/6023

Southard, J. (2022). Science of reading—decodable text for beginning readers. https://funinfirst.com/the-science-of-reading-decodable-text-for-beginning-readers/#:~:text=Decodable%20text%20falls%20under%20the,help%20them%20do%20just%20that!

TeacherVision Staff. (2019, November 15). Effective teachers think out loud on a regular basis. https://www.teachervision.com/problem-solving/think-aloud-strategy

Tompkins, G. E. (2014). *Literacy for the twenty first century: A balanced approach* (6th ed.). Pearson.

Tompkins, G. E. (2017). *Literacy for the twenty first century: A balanced approach* (7th ed.). Pearson.

Trevino, C. (2015, September 2). 7 qualities of great beginning reader books. Real Life at Home. https://www.reallifeathome.com/7-qualities-of-great-beginning-reader-books/

Walton, L. (2020, June 16). Using morning messages to start the day in distance learning. Edtopia. https://www.edutopia.org/article/using-morning-messages-start-day-distance-learning

Warley, H. P., Landrum, T. J., & Invernizzi, M. A. (2005). Prediction of first grade reading achievement: A comparison of kindergarten predictors. In B. Maloch, J. V. Hoffman, D. L. Schallert, C. M. Fairbanks, & J. Worthy (Eds.), *54th yearbook of the National Reading Conference* (pp. 428–442). National Reading Conference.

Weakland, M. (2020, July 27). Text for teaching beginning readers: Real, connected, authentic, decodable. *Mark Weakland Literacy*. https://www.markweaklandliteracy.com/blog/text-for-teaching-beginning-readers-real-connected-authentic-decodable

Wollacott, M. (2022, June 5). What are the different types of vocabulary? LanguageHumanities.org. https://www.languagehumanities.org/what-are-the

-different-types-of-vocabulary.htm#:~:text=There%20are%20four%20main%20types,develops%20with%20age%20and%20learning

Zemelman, S., Daniels, H., & Hyde, A. A. (2012). *Best practice: Bringing standards to life in America's classrooms*. Heinemann.

Chapter 4

Transitional Stage

Janet Deck

At the end of his first-grade year, Paxton was an average reader. He met the standards for first grade, but reading had not yet "clicked" for him. At the start of summer, his parents modeled the talk-to-text feature on their devices when searching for videos to play for Paxton and his younger sister. Picking up on this technique, Paxton soon started searching for kids' videos that he wanted to watch by using the talk-to-text feature. As he saw the spoken words become print, he started recognizing those printed words in other places (e.g., environmentally printed instructional signs at theme parks and restaurants). By the end of the summer before he started second grade, Paxton was reading "everything," according to his parents. He was excited to show off his newfound skill and was reading to everyone who would listen. Furthermore, Paxton was excited about second grade and was confident as he entered a new school year.

ANTICIPATION GUIDE

Read the following four statements before reading the chapter. Decide if you agree or disagree with each statement. Then read the chapter. After reading the chapter revisit the anticipation guide and decide if your views are the same or have changed.

1. During the Transitional period of reading development, students have mastered all phonics skills.
2. At the Transitional stage of development as a writer, students are beginning to engage in the writing process.

3. Diphthongs and digraphs are synonyms that identify the same phonological units.
4. Students in the Transitional period of word knowledge development are proficient with inflectional suffixes.

CHARACTERISTICS OF THE TRANSITIONAL STAGE

The Transitional stage is an exciting time in the life of a child. During this stage, reading starts to make sense. Usually this developmental period starts at the end of first grade or the beginning of second grade, but sometimes this development may not start until as late as the beginning of fourth grade. During the Transitional stage, oral reading rate increases from 29 or fewer words per minute (wpm) to 40 to 70+ wpm with an accuracy rate of 95 percent. As a reader, the child typically has a large bank of sight words, starting around 150 at the beginning of the Transitional stage and ending at approximately 400 words. Also, the Transitional reader understands spelling patterns and can use these to decode unknown words. Typical Transitional students can spell single-syllable, short vowel words; words with beginning consonant digraphs; and two-letter consonant blends. Students use spelling patterns that they have mastered to encode words as they write. However, not all phonics skills have been mastered. Therefore, another name for Transitional readers is within-word pattern spellers (Gehsmann & Templeton, 2022).

TRANSITIONAL READERS

At the Transitional stage, students are within the Developmental Reading Assessment (DRA) levels of 14 to 24 and Guided Reading Levels H to L (Fountas & Pinnell, 2018) and are learning how to decode vowel teams, such as "oo," "ea," and "ou"; vowel teams consist of two or more adjacent vowels that represent only one sound. Transitional readers are also learning how to decode vowel diphthongs such as "oi," "oy," and "ow."

Diphthongs

Diphthongs can be tricky because they are two adjacent vowels that start as one sound and go into another in the same syllable. Diphthongs are also known as "gliding vowels" because one sound literally glides quickly into the other sound. In addition to digraphs and diphthongs, the Transitional reader is learning regularly spelled two-syllable words with long and short vowel sounds and silent letter combinations, such as "know," "lamb," "ghost," and "guess" (Florida Department of Education, 2022).

Sight Words

Sight words, words known by sight and not by decoding, have evolved since Edward Dolch's (1936) first study on what words children know in first grade. In his seminal study, Dolch's guiding principles included words known as opposed to words used, words children used as a result of experience, words with a degree of meaning, and words that were known to a definite percentage of children. Currently, the Dolch sight word list comprises 315 words divided into grade categories from pre-K to grade 3 (Bales, 2019).

Another common list of sight words was developed by Edward Fry in 1957 and revised in 1980. Fry named his list "instant words" because students need to recognize them instantly. The Fry lists were created in conjunction with the curriculum and followed the principles of "what are the most useful words students need to know" followed by "what are the next most useful words students need to know" (Fry, 1980). Currently, the Fry list contains 1,000 words categorized by level, from first to tenth. However, students should have all 1,000 words mastered by grade 5 (K12 Reader, 2022).

Comprehension

As Transitional students develop fluency, their text comprehension also increases; however, comprehension strategies should be explicitly taught so that students' engagement increases and they become more efficient in listening and silent reading comprehension. Explicit instruction in before-, during-, and after-reading strategies will cultivate this active construction of meaning. Typical before-reading strategies may include activating background knowledge, identifying unfamiliar vocabulary, and making predictions. During reading, students need to be able to draw inferences, make connections to the text, summarize what they have read, and generate questions for clarification. After reading, Transitional readers should be able to retell the text, including main ideas and supporting concepts, and make connections to and beyond the text. By scaffolding teaching of before-, during-, and after-reading strategies, students will become efficient using these comprehension strategies for engagement and implement them during their independent silent reading (Gehsmann & Templeton, 2022).

CHARACTERISTICS OF TRANSITIONAL TEXT

As students enter the Transitional period, children will be comfortable independently reading texts with which they are familiar. Texts such as the Pete the Cat series by James Dean (2010) or *Goodnight, Moon* by Margaret Wise Brown (1947) are books that children have experienced as read alouds multiple times; therefore these texts are good choices for independent reading for students entering the Transitional phase.

As children advance to the middle of the Transitional phase, they develop increased reading stamina, enhanced fluency, and a broader base of sight words. Typically, they can read books with about 50 pages containing up to six sentences per page. Transitional readers may enjoy exploring the simple chapter book series by Cynthia Rylant (1996), Henry and Mudge, a comical narrative about a boy and his 180-pound dog. Another appealing series for Transitional readers is Nate the Great by Marjorie Sharmat (1977). Nate is a pancake-eating boy detective who loves to solve mysteries. Learners in the Transitional stage are ready to master additional literary elements in addition to characters, setting, conflict, and resolution; additional learning may also include flashbacks and foreshadowing. These additional elements may be challenging at first, but students will enjoy the added layers of meaning.

Toward the end of the Transitional stage of reading, students develop the ability to read increasingly complex text with less support from illustrations, more sentences per page, and more pages to the text. Students in the Transitional stage encounter complex elements such as metaphors, figurative language, and wordplay. Informational texts also increase in complexity, and students need to learn how to use text features in order to increase their understanding. By the end of this period, Transitional readers need considerable amounts of time to read. As much as possible, allowing students to choose their books, even in a controlled choice, can contribute to reading motivation, stamina, fluency, and comprehension (Gehsmann & Templeton, 2022).

TRANSITIONAL WRITERS

As a writer, a student in the Transitional period can write for meaning by composing paragraphs and may be able to write responses to reading. They start to recognize morphological concepts and incorporate base words and affixes into their writing. Students' writing becomes more descriptive, and they start varying their sentence length. At this stage, Transitional writers are also starting to engage in the writing process, including drafting, revising, and editing of narrative texts (Gehsmann & Templeton, 2022).

Because of the increase in writing during the Transitional stage of writing development, students need to be able to incorporate an increased use of appropriate writing conventions. Whereas Transitional students should already have mastered simple conventions such as capitalizing proper nouns and subject-verb agreement in simple sentences, more advanced concepts such as use of possessives, forming plurals by changing the final "-y" to "ies," and regular inflectional suffixes are mastered by the end of this stage (Florida Department of Education, 2022). During this stage, learners are developing the ability to conjugate regular and irregular verbs. Transitional readers start using regular and irregular plural nouns in their writing, and students use simple modifiers while maintaining consistent verb tenses across paragraphs (Florida Department of Education, 2022).

At the Transitional stage of writing development, handwriting instruction and practice are essential. Many students at this age are learning cursive writing. The goal of handwriting instruction is for students to write fluently and legibly so that they can cognitively focus on the content of their writing, structure, and spelling. During the Transitional period, students benefit from writing by hand more than writing with a computer. Writing by hand only requires one hand to write, whereas typing on a computer requires two hands. Typing with two hands requires cognitive development to allow communication between both hemispheres of the brain, and Transitional learners do not yet have the brain maturity for two-handed typing efficiency (Gehsmann & Templeton, 2022).

Importantly, students' development during the Transitional stage can vary in length. While some students may move quickly through this period, others may need more time for the concepts to make sense. Multiple researchers (Flanagan et al., 2011; Spichtig et al., 2019) have demonstrated that readers who struggle later in school do so because they did not master concepts in the Transitional period of development. The bottom line is not to rush children through this stage of development. Monitor student progress and provide interventions designed for students to develop the necessary characteristics of a Transitional reader and writer.

FAIRY TALES

The genre of fairy tale is popular with Transitional readers because of the familiarity of the story, the element of magic, and the resolution of "happily ever after." For the Transitional reader, this genre has easily identifiable story elements—beginning, middle, ending—as well as easily identifiable characters, setting, conflict, and resolution.

Fairy tales also have multiple versions of the same story. For example, *The Gingerbread Man* (1998) by Jim Aylesworth and *The Ninjabread Man* by C. J. Leigh (2016) are similar stories. Most students are familiar with the traditional story of the gingerbread man. *The Gingerbread Man* by Aylesworth is a classic retelling of the original fairy tale, replete with fun rhyme schemes, and Aylesworth's book is filled with colorful illustrations by Barbara McClintock, serving to engage young readers. *The Ninjabread Man* by Leigh is a derivative of the classic tale. In *The Ninjabread Man*, Sensei is the character who makes the recipe for "ninjabread," but the "Ninjabread Man" escapes from the oven just as in the original fairy tale. Ninjabread Man runs into other "ninja" characters during his adventure, eventually being outsmarted by Ninja Fox.

Story Map

A story map is a graphic organizer designed to identify key elements of a narrative text. Typically, a basic story map for Transitional readers provides a framework for identifying the beginning, middle, and end of the story. These maps help students develop a deeper understanding of how stories are organized so they can apply the understanding to other texts. A more advanced story map may include characters and setting or even conflict and resolution (Reading Rockets, 2022).

Closed Compare/Contrast Graphic Organizer

The two varieties of the classic version of *The Gingerbread Man* serve as paired texts that can be used to identify story elements and then applied to a writing activity to compare and contrast the stories. Creating a story map for each story as a during-reading strategy dovetails nicely to provide the foundation for completing a closed compare/contrast graphic organizer for the two texts. Because students have already identified story elements, they will be able to identify the similarities and differences between the stories. In a closed compare/contrast the teacher identifies the categories to be compared. These categories might include setting, characters, problem, and solution. In an open compare/contrast the students determine the categories.

EASY CHAPTER BOOKS

At the Transitional phase of reading, students are starting to enjoy easy chapter books. They may even be able to start reading easy chapter books silently for enjoyment. A traditional easy chapter book for use in this stage is *Charlotte's Web* by E. B. White (1952). This classic children's novel follows the life of Wilbur, a runt pig saved by Fern, an empathetic eight-year-old daughter of a farmer. In the barn, Wilbur is introduced to Charlotte, a barn spider who lives in the rafters. Charlotte comes up with a plan to save Wilbur from becoming Christmas dinner. Even though the book embraces some difficult topics, including fear and loneliness, E. B. White's writing is humorous and engaging, a perfect combination for Transitional readers.

SWBS

The post-reading strategy of Somebody Wanted But So (SWBS) by Macon et al. (1991) is a simple strategy for students to use to create a summary of a narrative or expository text. The steps include first identifying the "somebody." It should be pointed out that there can be multiple "somebodies" since most stories include multiple characters. The second column, "wanted," represents the plot of the story or the motivation of the character. Just like the "character" element, there may be multiple "wants" by the character(s). The "but" component is the conflict, and "so" is the resolution. When teaching this summarizing strategy, modeling SWBS will get students motivated to contribute multiple SWBSes they identify throughout the text. For example, Wilbur (**somebody**) **wanted** to be saved from Christmas dinner, **but** he didn't know how, **so** he cried in the corner of the barn. Another example could be Charlotte (**somebody**) **wanted** to save Wilbur, **but** she was very small and couldn't get attention, **so** she wove special words about Wilbur in her web.

SWBST

Multiple variations of SWBS have been published to add additional story elements to the summary. One popular variation is Somebody Wanted But So Then (SWBST). This adaptation adds "then," an overall outcome/resolution. Modifying the first example to a SWBST could be Wilbur (**somebody**) **wanted** to be saved from Christmas dinner, **but** he didn't know how, **so** he cried in the corner of the barn; **then,** Wilbur met Charlotte, a barn spider, who used her web to spin words about Wilbur's characteristics.

SWBSF

Another modification to SWBS is Somebody Wanted But So Then Finally (SWBSTF). Again, SWBSTF is just a more advanced summary to be used when students are capable of adding to a summary statement to indicate additional details. If we continue the first SWBS example, SWBSTF could be

Wilbur (**somebody**) **wanted** to be saved from Christmas dinner, **but** he didn't know how, **so** he cried in the corner of the barn; **then,** Wilbur met Charlotte, a barn spider, who used her web to spin words about Wilbur's characteristics. **Finally,** Mr. Zuckerman recognizes Wilbur's special uniqueness and Wilbur's life is spared.

POV RESPONSE

A partner writing strategy to SWBS is teaching point of view (POV). POV can be simple, such as teaching first-, second-, and third-person views, or POV instruction can be more complex, such as teaching students that everyone has a different perspective. Having a different perspective may mean that not everyone agrees. Teaching students to disagree respectfully is an important element of social emotional learning.

Since students have already used SWBS to summarize story lines from *Charlotte's Web*, they are familiar with different POVs from the characters in the text. The first conflict appears when Mr. Arable and Fern disagree about what to do with the runt pig. Mr. Arable, a seasoned farmer, knows that the runt pig cannot live without its mother's milk, but because it's so small, the runt pig isn't strong enough to suckle. He intended to kill the runt mercifully so it would not starve to death. Fern loudly disagreed with Mr. Arable's decision. As an eight-year-old, Fern could not understand how her father could kill a sweet little pig, even after Mr. Arable explained the "why" of his decision. Mr. Arable and Fern came to a decision that was agreeable to both characters.

Students will probably read the conflicting POVs and take Fern's POV. However, it would be interesting to have them voice whether or not they agree with Fern's method of communicating her desire to keep the runt pig alive. Do they agree with her demanding, temper-tantrum tactics? If so, why? If not, why not? How would they have communicated their message to Mr. Arable? Having students write their POVs in response to other POVs represented in the text will engage Transitional writers as well as teach them about respectful disagreement.

FANTASY

The genre of fantasy in children's literature is popular among children because of its use of magic. Elementary children are enamored with magic, and fantasy literature incorporates magic as well as fantastical characters, mythical worlds, and even dangerous quests. It is easy for elementary children to engage in fantasy because they love to play pretend; many times their pretend play incorporates magical powers.

The example text in the fantasy genre is *Tell Me a Dragon* by Morris (2009). In this beautifully illustrated book, Morris presents a fantastical world in which each person has their own unique dragon. The dragons represent the needs or personalities of the individual. With minimal text on each page, this book is perfect for the strategy of repeated reading.

Buddy Reading

A fluency strategy, repeated reading (Samuels, 1979), helps students develop accuracy and automaticity. The simple strategy incorporates multiple oral readings of the same text. Buddy reading is a form of repeated reading with the addition of using pairs to repeatedly read the text to one another (see table 4.1).

For buddy reading, divide the class into pairs. Each member of the pair reads one section of the text orally three times. The first time the student reads the text to the partner, the other student does not comment on the reading. The second time, the buddy who is listening identifies an area where the reader has improved since the first reading. The first partner reads the text a third time and after listening to their peer again comments on an area of improvement. The students then switch roles, and the listener becomes the reader. The second student reads the next passage three times, and each time the listener completes the rubric looking for areas of improvement. This approach helps to keep the feedback and attitudes positive, thus building self-confidence.

An added benefit of buddy reading is that students also increase their comprehension of text due to multiple exposures to the same text. Because the example text, *Tell Me a Dragon* by Morris, has common sight words as well as some advanced vocabulary for Transitional readers (e.g., "perfumed,"

Table 4.1 Buddy Reading

After 2nd Read	After 3rd Read	Buddy Reading
		Remembered more words
		Read faster
		Read smoother
		Read with greater expression

"snaggle-toothed"), sight words will be reinforced, and students will increase their vocabularies of multisyllabic words with repeated readings.

The example text is a stunning illustration of descriptive, fantastical writing. As students repeatedly read this book, they are exposed to vivid descriptions of multiple dragons with corresponding illustrations. At the end of the book, Morris incorporates "Field Notes and Observations on the Lives and Habits of Dragons." This text feature presents specific dragon "facts," including their skin, feathers, eggs, and magical powers.

Field Notes with Pictures

As a corresponding writing strategy, students should create their own personal dragons, describing features such as size, colors, and magical powers, and write an additional page to Morris's book, incorporating their text and illustrations. Students should incorporate what they learned about dragons from the "Field Notes and Observations" section as well as the main text. Because elementary students are naturally drawn to magical powers, incorporating this descriptive writing technique will engage them in reading, writing, and illustrating.

MYSTERY

The genre of mystery literature incorporates ordinary story elements such as characters, setting, plot, conflict, and resolution. However, it also incorporates plot twists, false leads, foreshadowing, a crime solver, a villain, and an eleventh-hour resolution to the crime. Kids love to play detective, looking for clues and solving mysteries, making this genre a Transitional reader favorite.

The example texts for this genre are in a series by Gertrude Chandler Warner (1942) called The Boxcar Children. Warner, an elementary teacher motivated to give students engaging literature, published her first Boxcar book in 1924. Because of its popularity, she wrote an additional 18 Boxcar books in her series prior to her death in 1979. Scholastic started adding to the Boxcar series in 1991 using ghostwriters, and currently there are 150+ Boxcar books.

The main characters in the Boxcar series are four orphaned brothers and sisters who are trying to stay together. They live in a train boxcar and encounter many mysteries, which they successfully solve. The Boxcar children are endearing characters, each with unique and relatable personalities, and Transitional readers are able to connect with the main characters, rooting for them to stay together and solve each mystery.

Text Talk

A during-reading strategy developed by Beck and McKeown (2001), text talk gives students opportunities to deconstruct language strategically. This strategy also aligns with the Science of Reading due to the enhancement of vocabulary and text comprehension. The procedures of text talk incorporate teacher-developed, open-ended critical thinking questions. Students can discuss the questions in pairs or groups and give a response orally or in writing. However, the focus of the strategy is talking. When students are talking, they are interacting with language, which forces them to interact with vocabulary. By discussing the text with a partner or group, students increase their comprehension of the text.

First-Person Journals

Using journals as a response to reading can take many forms. A common literature response journal is a first-person journal in which the student assumes a character from the reading and writes an entry as though they were that character. Using journals as a response to literature prompts imagination and motivation while developing critical thinking skills (Gunning, 2020).

In a first-person journal, students answer prompts as the characters as they develop throughout the book. For example, in our example text, The Boxcar Children by Warner (1942), the four main characters are the two brothers and two sisters (i.e., Henry, Jessie, Violet, and Benny) who are trying to stay together after their parents pass away. As the children encounter mysteries and problem-solve their day-to-day difficulties, their character traits grow and change. Students can journal about the characters' growth. Example character journal prompts may include: What characteristics do you have that will help you overcome the problem? What did you do to help solve the problem? Did anyone help you? By having students follow the development of a character in an engaging text, they are increasing their writing skills and critical thinking/problem-solving skills at the same time.

SELF-HELP

Children are not born knowing how to manage their emotions, share their toys, or get along well with other children. These skills need to be developed. When a child has developed social emotional learning (also known as social emotional literacy), they have fewer emotional disruptions and less emotional stress (Palmer, 2019). Schools can help with teaching skills to develop social emotional literacy.

While many tools to support social emotional learning are implemented in a school-wide setting such as antibullying campaigns and positive behavior supports, using self-help books as read alouds is an easy and fun way to integrate social emotional literacy. Many good read alouds promote social emotional concepts. Consider incorporating *Your Name Is a Song* by Jamilah Thompkins-Bigelow (2021), *Star Knights* (a graphic novel) by Kay Davault (2022), and *The More You Give* by Marcy Campbell (2022).

The example text for the genre of self-help for Transitional readers is *How Full Is Your Bucket? (for Kids)* by Tom Rath (2009). This sweet text for children follows a day in the life of Felix, an elementary school child who becomes aware, through an interaction with his grandpa, that everyone has an invisible bucket. Daily experiences and events either add water drops or take away drops. At first Felix becomes aware of his own bucket, but as the day goes along he becomes aware of others' buckets and even questions whether his pet dog has his own bucket. Felix's journey to self-awareness and his contribution to filling others' buckets leads to his increased social emotional literacy.

Think-Pair-Share

The think-pair-share strategy (Lyman, 1981), originally listen-think-pair-share, was developed by Lyman as a way for teachers to incorporate think time after posing a question. Initially, the listen-think-pair-share was a response strategy to a read aloud, and Lyman's study focused on first graders. Over the years, however, the strategy has grown and changed slightly. The original focus of the strategy was on wait time (ten seconds from the point of question). Lyman posited that increased wait time produced longer and more elaborate answers than without an increase in wait time after posing a question. The results of the Lyman study included an increase in inferences with supportive evidence, increase in student discussion participation, and increase in logical argument. By adding the element of collaboration (pair), student verbal interaction increased, which also promoted positive effects on achievement and attitude.

The procedures for think-pair-share (Lyman, 1981) are relatively simple. The teacher can present a read aloud or students can be assigned a portion of text to read silently. Strategically, the teacher will present a critical thinking question. Students will "**think**" about their responses to the question; Lyman suggests giving them ten seconds. After "think" time, students will discuss their thoughts with their partners (pair). When the "**pair**" time ends, students then "**share**" their thoughts with a larger group. The share time does not always have to be oral sharing. Lyman suggested that sharing responses can be written or diagrammed. Furthermore, Lyman indicated that teachers may give more elaborate instructions in addition to a question. Teachers may want to add elements such as consensus-building or problem-solving.

The example text, *How Full Is Your Bucket? (for Kids)* by Rath, can first be used as a read aloud to present to the entire class. Because this example text focuses on Felix's social emotional development, Rath presents a problem that Felix solves throughout the course of his day. Having think-pair-share prompts/questions at strategic points throughout the reading of the text can help students to be socially aware of themselves as well as others. This book is also one that can prompt students to think of situations in which they, like Felix, had their "buckets" emptied or filled. These situations could be considered as one of the "paired" discussions.

SEL Writing Prompt

Developing social emotional literacy (SEL) extends to classroom management and developing classroom community. Using books from the self-help genre can serve as a foundation for your SEL instruction, with many easy-to-implement writing strategies. Using our mentor text, *How Full Is Your Bucket? (for Kids)* by Rath, a quick search of teacherspayteachers.com resulted in multiple freebies. A specific example of a "bucket filler" prompt by Lindsay Sauer (n.d.) includes having students recognize why their bucket was filled and who filled it (http://sweetnsauerfirsties.com/category/uncategorized/). Another "bucket filler" prompt that teaches students to identify cause and effect is by Hatchet (n.d.) on teacherspayteachers.com. Hatchet has students identify the bucket filler/bucket spiller prompt and the effect it had on the character. For example, Felix would not play with Anna, so Anna knocked down Felix's block tower. Using SEL writing prompts in response to literature reinforces positive character traits, helps students identify negative behaviors, and provides problem-solving strategies to help avoid the negative behavior.

ANTICIPATION GUIDE REVISITED

At the beginning of the chapter, you examined four statements. Based upon what you have read in this chapter, revisit the anticipation guide statements and decide if your views are the same or have changed.

1. During the Transitional period of reading development, students have mastered all phonics skills.
2. At the Transitional stage of development as a writer, students are beginning to engage in the writing process.

3. Diphthongs and digraphs are synonyms that identify the same phonological units.
4. Students in the Transitional period of word knowledge development are proficient with inflectional suffixes.

CONCLUSION

At the beginning of this chapter, Paxton's "aha" moments of his journey into the Transitional reading stage illustrated how he became enamored with how words made sense. He applied his own spoken words as they appeared in print to words he identified in his environment. The more he saw his words, the more he was able to apply them, thus increasing his sight word vocabulary and his ability to decode unknown words. As Paxton enters second grade, it is relatively easy to see how he is excited to explore the genres in this chapter and how he will develop as a reader through the instructional strategies presented. The engaging strategies and the displayed characteristics of the Transitional reader provide opportunities for meaningful learning.

STOP AND THINK

1. Identify a specific Transitional level text for which you could have your students construct a first-person journal. Explain the characteristics of the text (qualitative, quantitative, and reader and text) that make it appropriate for Transitional readers. Identify five specific prompts that you would have students respond to in their journals as though they are one of the characters in the text.
2. Identify two texts on the same topic. Provide the title and author of each. These could be two similar fairy tales or an informational and a narrative text on the same topic. Create a closed compare/contrast graphic organizer. Explain what categories you chose and your rationale for choosing those categories.
3. Based on the strategies described in this chapter, identify additional strategies you have discovered that you could use in your instruction for Transitional readers and writers. Explain how and when you would use them.

REFERENCES

Aylesworth, J. (1998). *The gingerbread man.* Scholastic.

Bales, K. (2019, July 12). What are Fry words? Learn how they compare to Dolch sight words. Thought Co. https://www.thoughtco.com/what-are-fry-words-4172325

Beck, I., & McKeown, M. (2001). Text talk: Capturing the benefits of read-aloud experiences for young children. *The reading teacher*, *55*(1), 10.

Brown, M. W. (1947). *Goodnight, moon*. Harper & Row.

Campbell, M (2022). *The more you give*. Random House Children's Books.

Davault, K. (2022) *Star knights* (a graphic novel). Random House Graphic.

Dean, J. (2010). *Pete the cat*. HarperCollins.

Dolch, E. W. (1936). How much word knowledge do children bring to grade one? *The Elementary English Review*, *13*(5), 177–183. https://www.jstor.org/stable/41383019

Flanagan, K., Hayes, L., Templeton, S., Bear, D. R., Invernizzi, M., & Johnston, F. (2011). *Words their way with struggling readers: Word study for reading, vocabulary, and spelling instruction grades 4–12*. Pearson/Allyn & Bacon.

Florida Department of Education. (2022). Florida's B.E.S.T. standards English language arts. https://www.fldoe.org/core/fileparse.php/7539/urlt/elabeststandardsfinal.pdf

Fountas & Pinnell. (2018, June 12). Fountas & Pinnell reading levels. *Building Momentum in Schools*. https://buildingmomentuminschools.blog/2018/06/12/fountas-pinnell-reading-levels/

Fry, E. (1980). The new instant word list. *The Reading Teacher*, *34*(3), 284–289. http://www.jstor.org/stable/20195230

Gehsmann, K., & Templeton, S. (2022). *Teaching reading and writing: The developmental approach*. Pearson.

Gunning, T. (2020). *Creating literacy instruction for all*. Pearson.

Hatchet. S. (n.d.). How to fill your bucket. *Teachers Pay Teachers*. https://www.teacherspayteachers.com/Product/How-Full-is-Your-Bucket-3204858?st=ee696a3377058e01c94370176c16cf4f

K12 Reader. (2022). Fry word list: 1,000 high frequency words. https://www.k12reader.com/subject/vocabulary/fry-words/

Kuhn, M., Schwanenflugel, P., Morris, R., Morrow, L., Woo, D., Meisinger, E., Sevcik, R., Bradley, B., & Stahl, S. (2006). Teaching children to become fluent and automatic readers. *Journal of Literacy Research*, *38*(4), 357–387.

Leigh, C. J. (2016). *The ninjabread man*. Orchard Books.

Lyman, F. (1981). The responsive classroom discussion. In A. S. Anderson (Ed.), *Mainstreaming digest*, 109–113. University of Maryland College of Education.

Macon, J., Bewell, D., & Vogt, M. (1991). *Responses to literature: Grades K to 8*. International Reading Association.

Morris, J. (2009). *Tell me a dragon*. Frances Lincoln Children's Books.

Palmer, J. (2019, October 9). Social and emotional development in early learning settings. NCSL. https://www.ncsl.org/research/human-services/social-and-emotional-development-in-early-learning-settings.aspx

Rasinski, T. V., Reutzel, D. R., Chard, D., & Linan-Thompson, S. (2011). Reading fluency. In M. L. Kamil, P. D. Pearson, E. B. Moje, & P. P. Afflerbach (Eds.), *Handbook of reading research*, *IV* (pp. 286–319). Routledge.

Rath, T. (2009). *How full is your bucket? (for kids).* Gallup Press.
Reading Rockets. (2022). Story maps. https://www.readingrockets.org/strategies/story_maps
Rylant, C. (1996). *Henry and Mudge.* Simon & Schuster.
Samuels, S. J. (1979). The method of repeated readings. *The Reading Teacher, 32*(4), 403–408.
Sauer, L. (n.d.). Sweet 'n' sauer firsties. http://sweetnsauerfirsties.com/categity/uncategorized/
Sharmat, M. (1977). *Nate the great.* Random House Children's Books.
Spichtig, A., Gehsmann, K., Pascoe, J., & Ferrara, J. (2019). The impact of adaptive, web-based, scaffolded silent reading instruction on the reading achievement of students in grades 4 and 5. *The Elementary School Journal, 119*(3), 443–467. https://doi.org/10.1086/701705
Thompkins-Bigelow, J. (2021). *Your name is a song.* Innovation Press.
Warner, G. C. (1942). *The boxcar children.* Albert Whitman & Company.
White, E. B. (1952). *Charlotte's web.* Harper and Brothers.

Chapter 5

Intermediate Stage

Janet Deck

Knowing that her fifth-grade class would be exploring many types of informational texts, Mrs. Kay starts the school year with a text feature scavenger hunt. Because informational texts can be overwhelming to some students, making a game of the text features helps students preview the text and their learning throughout the school year. Mrs. Kay partners students together and has them examine their science textbook. Students need to identify simple elements such as title and table of contents and more difficult elements such as graphs, tables, photographs, headings, subheadings, and hyperlinks. In addition to the identification of the text features, students must indicate the page on which they found the feature and how it helps them understand the information in the text. To culminate the activity, students identify which was the most exciting text feature they found and why it was so exciting. For example, one group was mesmerized by the chapter on astronomy, weather, and climate. The students noted that the illustrations of the solar system, along with the sidebar that gave information about the planetary orbits and distance to the sun, were particularly interesting. Another collaborative group was animated in their description of the bison and the ecosystems of Yellowstone National Park referenced in the chapter on living things and their environments. One of the students had been on a family vacation to the grasslands of Greater Yellowstone and had seen bison. The student shared his experiences and connected his learning for the group, thus creating additional background knowledge for the other learners. This prereading activity, also known as a text feature walk, created a classroom "buzz" that engaged students in their anticipated science learning, taking away the anxiety of reading a difficult text.

ANTICIPATION GUIDE

Read the following statements before reading the chapter. Decide if you agree or disagree with each statement. Then read the chapter. After reading the chapter, revisit the anticipation guide and decide if your views are the same or have changed.

1. During the Intermediate stage, children can solve problems in a logical fashion; however, they are typically not able to think abstractly or hypothetically.
2. By the end of the Intermediate stage, readers are reading at the same rate as average adult readers.
3. Derivational suffixes change the tense or quantity of a word.
4. At the Intermediate stage of development, students are able to write an essay with a central theme using multiple sources for support.

CHARACTERISTICS OF INTERMEDIATE READERS

Intermediate students, typically in grades 3 through 5, have reached the concrete operational stage of development (Piaget, 2000). In this cognitive stage, even though children's thinking is still concrete, it becomes more logical and organized. While they are progressing, abstract and hypothetical concepts still may be a struggle. Students in the concrete operational stage become aware that their thoughts, feelings, and opinions are unique to themselves. These changes are significant to learners' development as Intermediate readers. Literacy develops in a social context, and students in third through fifth grades begin to see the world more broadly than in previous years (Piaget, 2000). Intermediate students begin to develop a deeper understanding of others' points of view as they are learning to connect to historical perspectives. They are developing the ability to analyze the differences between the narrator's point of view and a character's perspective (Florida Department of Education, 2022).

At the Intermediate stage of reading, students' reading rate increases to approximately 100 to 145 wpm, while adult readers have an average reading rate of 200 to 250 wpm. These upper elementary learners prefer to read silently, and their expanded vocabulary facilitates their ability to engage reflectively with increasingly complex texts. Increases in development and skills promote "staying power," the ability of students to stay engaged in a text for extended periods of time (Gehsmann & Templeton, 2022).

Decoding Multisyllabic Words

Intermediate readers are secure in their foundational knowledge of word and single-syllable patterns, allowing them to extend this awareness to patterns in multisyllabic words. Single-syllable words are easily read and spelled. However, students may still need instruction on ambiguous vowels that are neither long nor short (Pearson Education, 2009). Intermediate students are also becoming more aware of morphology, how words are put together.

Inflectional Suffixes

During the Transitional stage, learners mastered inflectional suffixes, which created a new form of a word by changing the number or tense of the root word. These suffixes included adding an "-s" or "-es," which changed the word to the plural form, and adding "-ed" or "-ing," which changed the tense. During the Intermediate stage, they are developing an understanding of common derivational suffixes such as "-ful," "-less," and "-est" and their impact on the part of speech. Instead of changing the number or tense, derivational affixes change the grammatical category. The derivational suffix "-ly" transforms an adjective into an adverb, while the suffix "-ment" changes a verb to a noun (English Language Linguistics, n.d.). This increase in language development facilitates advanced general academic vocabulary and domain-specific terminology (Gehsmann & Templeton, 2022).

Students at the Intermediate stage will profit from increased instruction to support textual comprehension. During this stage, these learners are developing confidence in identifying a variety of text structures: chronology, comparison, cause/effect, problem/solution, sequence, and descriptive text structures (Florida Department of Education, 2022). They are also learning to compare and evaluate information presented from primary and secondary sources on the same topic (Florida Department of Education, 2022).

Primary and Secondary Sources

Because much of the Intermediate stage of reading focuses on informational texts, students need to learn the difference between primary and secondary sources. Primary sources "bring the past to life" (Gunning, 2020, p. 426). These sources include diaries, letters, memoirs, and even drawings—evidence created by those who participated in the event. In addition, primary sources include published peer-reviewed research that is factual, not interpretive. On the other hand, secondary sources are secondhand accounts of the event. For upper elementary students, reading primary sources teaches them how to understand and interpret the past, helping them to think like historians or scientists (Gunning, 2020).

Figurative Language

As students engage with literature and informational text, they should be taught to consider the genre, which affects the way they read, including what they do before, during, and after reading. Through reading narrative texts, they are learning to analyze how setting, events, conflict, and characterization contribute to plot development (Florida Department of Education, 2022). They are also developing an understanding of figurative language. During the Intermediate stage, learners are exposed to six of the types of figurative language (metaphors, similes, alliterations, personifications, hyperboles, and idioms); the rest of the twelve types will be developed in later stages. Metaphors and similes are comparisons between two things. Similes use "like" or "as," while metaphors do not. Alliteration involves the repetition of the same sound (frequently a consonant) at the beginning of a series of words. Giving human qualities to something that is not human is personification. Hyperbole involves exaggerating something in a humorous way. An example is "His smile was a mile wide when he saw his lost love." Idioms are expressions whose meaning cannot be understood by the individual words. An example is "It was raining cats and dogs" (Betts, n.d.).

When reading informational texts, students should preview the passage, noting difficult vocabulary and thinking about what they may encounter. As they move through the text, Intermediate readers need to clarify any confusing information, questioning the text as they read. During this period, they begin comparing primary and secondary sources on the same topic and learn to track the development of a position by identifying specific claims, evidence, and reasoning (Florida Department of Education, 2022). The Claim-Evidence-Reasoning (C-E-R) framework (McNeill & Krajcik, 2011) is a strategy to get students thinking like scientists. Students make a claim, similar to a hypothesis. Then they must use evidence to support their claim and explain their reasoning. When teachers incorporate C-E-R, students develop an enhanced conceptual understanding and carefully analyze their claims by using evidence to support their reasonings. Whether reading literature or informational texts, students should summarize their reading, identifying the gist and importance of the passage. Teaching these basic strategies to Intermediate readers will support their development of critical reading skills (Gehsmann & Templeton, 2022).

CHARACTERISTICS OF TEXTS FOR INTERMEDIATE READERS

By the end of third grade, most students have mastered the foundational skills and are reading texts at Lexile levels between 645 and 860 (Dagen & Bean, 2020). However, by the end of third grade significant changes in how students read and write have developed. The fourth-grade year brings literature and informational texts that become increasingly complex in vocabulary, syntax, and concepts. In fourth and fifth grades, Intermediate readers are exposed to complex academic vocabulary and content-specific words. Devoting instructional time to teach those words will not only increase students' vocabulary, but text comprehension will also increase as students are able to understand those vocabulary words in context.

Syntax

In addition to complex vocabulary, the syntax becomes more complex as well. Syntax awareness helps students interact with the text by giving them the ability to chunk texts in order to make meaning at the sentence level. Therefore, teachers must teach students how to use syntax to aid with text comprehension (Mokhtari & Niederhauser, 2012). Oral sentence reading requires skills beyond those required to read word lists—even when the words in the lists and sentences are identical (Jenkins et al., 2003). The researchers determined that sentence reading was more predictive of reading comprehension than was word list reading. Students with specific reading comprehension deficits read word lists as well as comparison students did but performed more poorly than the control group on text reading fluency (Cutting et al., 2009).

As students learn more complex content, effective teachers teach students to connect new concepts to their existing knowledge base. Making concept connections promotes comprehension and builds motivation for further learning (Dagen & Bean, 2020).

Typically, books for Intermediate readers have fewer illustrations than books for Transitional readers, so Intermediate readers must rely on their understanding of text features to scaffold their comprehension. Texts in the fourth to fifth grades stretch band range between 740L and 1010L (EBSCO Connect, 2021). Importantly, some students in grades 3 through 5 may not yet have mastered foundational reading skills. These students will need continued small group instruction in foundational reading skills with emphasis on phonics and fluency (Dagen & Bean, 2020).

Academic Language

As texts for upper elementary students increase in complexity, teachers must increase explicit instruction in academic and content-specific vocabulary. Academic language refers to the language used in textbooks, school, and the workplace. This includes the key vocabulary words and concepts as well as the signal words and phrases. Understanding how signal words and phrases such as "even though" or "despite" are used in sentences is a key step in understanding the academic language students encounter, as well as a basis for using it correctly themselves (Breiseth, 2022). Content-specific vocabulary refers to vocabulary terms that are specific to a particular unit of study. This is the precise, content-specific vocabulary that is infused throughout the unit. These content vocabulary words are tier 3 vocabulary. These words are not a part of students' normal speaking vocabulary and need to be taught as part of the unit of study. In science, domain-specific words might include things like "hibernation," "nocturnal," and "hypothesis." Providing ample practice is important because it can take up to 17 exposures for children to move a new word into their long-term memory.

Structural Analysis

Teaching structural analysis strategies is an effective way for teachers to scaffold word study instruction. For example, when a student encounters an unfamiliar multisyllabic word, the student needs to understand how to divide it into morphemes, or units of meaning: affixes (both prefixes and suffixes), bases, and roots. At this stage, students should be taught affixes, units of meaning that are attached before (prefix) or after (suffix) a base or root word.

Base words are English words that can stand alone. For example, the word "uncomfortable" has the base word "comfort." The word "comfort" can stand alone as a word. However, the prefix "un-" and the suffix "-able" have been added to create a new word. A base word is different than a root word. A root word cannot stand alone; however, a root is a word part, usually Latin or Greek, that combines with affixes to form a word. For example, the Latin root "dorm" means "to sleep." Several words Intermediate readers may recognize come from this root word, such as "dormant," "dormancy," "dormitory," and "dormer." Even if students do not know the exact meaning of the words, they should be able to identify the Latin root "dorm" and deduce that the unknown words are connected to sleep. Using morphology to determine word meanings gives students a literacy tool to read complex vocabulary with understanding (Stahl et al., 2020).

Motivation

Researchers consistently note that motivation to read decreases as students enter the Intermediate stage of literacy (Guthrie et al., 2007). On average, 40% of students, sampled from 50 countries, reported being only "somewhat" or "less than" engaged in their reading lessons (Guthrie & Klauda, 2016). To address the issue of lack of motivation, allowing students to choose texts or activities as much as possible can promote student buy-in and stimulate motivation. For example, teachers can give students choice by a "this or that" vote. They may say something like, "This month we are going to read a new novel, but we are going to vote as a class on which one we will read." Then they can give a short presentation on each novel and allow the students to vote.

Another motivational strategy for Intermediate readers is peer collaboration. Meaningful interaction with peers can take many forms, but the essential element is socialization. Some strategies for peer collaboration are buddy reading, turn and talk, and collaborative learning. Allowing students to work together to comprehend a complex text will increase motivation and therefore increase learning (Dagen & Bean, 2020).

CHARACTERISTICS OF INTERMEDIATE WRITERS

As Intermediate writers, students are developing greater complexity as they write across genres. They are able to more fluently encode words and sentences, and they are able to use multiple sources to support their writing. During the Intermediate stage, students begin incorporating dialogue into their writing. In addition, as students are exposed to authors' craft techniques such as metaphor, allusion, and cliff-hangers, these elements will appear in their writing (Florida Department of Education, 2022). Overall, upper elementary students' writing becomes more interesting as they become engaged with their own writing.

Paraphrasing and Note-Taking

Because third through fifth graders are increasing their exposure to informational and expository texts, they need to become proficient at note-taking and paraphrasing. When reading or listening to information, students tend to try to write what they are exposed to verbatim. As they try to write exactly what they hear or read, their comprehension is interrupted, and their learning decreases. Paraphrasing is an essential skill for note-taking and involves writing the gist of the information presented. Paraphrasing needs to be modeled and then practiced. As teachers model the skill of paraphrasing, students will learn and put into practice paraphrasing information (Gehsmann & Templeton, 2022).

Writing Conventions

With an increase in writing at the Intermediate stage comes an increase in the need for instruction in writing conventions. During the Transitional stage, students started using regular and irregular plural nouns and simple modifiers. As they progress to the Intermediate stage, students should increase the complexity of their writing to include comparative and superlative adjectives. Instruction for mastery should be focused on recognition and correction of incorrect shifts in tense and number as well as appropriate use of conjunctions for correctly connecting words, phrases, and sentences (Florida Department of Education, 2022).

While students were exposed to the writing process during earlier years, upper elementary students are writing more extensively than Transitional writers; therefore, they need increased explicit instruction and practice with the writing process. The first phase of the writing process is planning, also known as prewriting. During this phase, students can brainstorm words, phrases, or concepts and use graphic organizers or mentor texts. Modeling the planning stage increases students' buy-in as they watch their teacher unfold the planning process. The drafting, or composing, stage is when most of the writing takes place. The first draft is messy, and students need to be taught that "messy" is expected. This part of the process is the place for students to experiment with language and the writer's craft. Teachers and peers give feedback, and writers develop as they apply that feedback. During the revising process, students implement the feedback they received during the drafting phase. This phase is where students revisit their drafts and make final decisions about their writing. Editing is the juncture at which students make spelling, mechanical, and grammatical revisions. The last part of the writing process is publishing. Students love to see their work published. Publishing their writing on a school website or another approved site for others to read can inspire students and encourage them to continue writing (Gehsmann & Templeton, 2022).

NONFICTION-INFORMATIONAL TEXTS

The example instructional text for the genre of nonfiction-informational is an engaging and beautifully illustrated book entitled *Molly Bannaky* by Alice McGill (1999). With minimal text per page and corresponding brilliant illustrations, this selection is a perfect read aloud. Students become engaged with the history presented because of its captivating and powerful characters. They root for Bannaky to be free, and they take up Molly's cause to survive in the "New World" as a young, single woman. While the text is fascinating, the best part of the book is the biographical information at the end. This page fills in the blanks about the significance of Molly Bannaky and her relationship to Benjamin Banneker, her grandson, the scientist and mathematician who was so highly regarded that he helped survey the planning of the city of Washington, D.C. In addition to the historical facts presented in the text, McGill skillfully writes about seemingly controversial issues, prompting students to desire further information. For example, in the beginning of the story, Molly was prosecuted for spilling a pail of milk. The usual penalty was death on the gallows, but Molly could read the Bible, so she was not killed. Students wonder why the penalty for spilling milk was so harsh. And how did Molly learn to read the Bible? Another common question relates to Molly and Bannaky marrying, even though it was against the law for a white woman to marry a black man. Why weren't they prosecuted? At the Intermediate stage of reading, students are curious and want to research their questions. *Molly Bannaky* opens lots of opportunities to investigate additional information.

Probable Passage

Originally, Wood (1984) developed the strategy of Probable Passage as a writing strategy for reluctant writers. The process began by the teacher identifying terms from a text, then students would categorize them based on how they expected the term to be used in the text. Students would then use their prior knowledge about grammar and composition to compose the narrative, thus giving teachers the opportunity to teach vocabulary and text comprehension in a single lesson. Beers (2003) adapted the technique of Probable Passage into a prereading strategy for engagement and text comprehension. Essentially, Beers created a graphic organizer that includes boxes for "characters, setting, problem, and outcomes." Students were to use what they know about story structure and vocabulary to take the list of Probable Passage words and place them in the appropriate Probable Passage box.

Through discussion with a partner or group, students must come up with a "gist statement," a prediction that tells the "gist" of what the text may be about. If the teacher chooses, students can fill out the Probable Passage independently or in groups. Beers includes a box for "unknown words," to be used if students genuinely do not understand a word. However, a good suggestion is to limit the number of words put in the "unknown words" box to avoid students saturating the box. The last section of the Probable Passage organizer is entitled "To discover . . . ". This section is for students to write questions they have about the text after they have interacted with the given vocabulary and developed their gist statements.

To apply Probable Passage to our mentor text, *Molly Bannaky*, consider giving students the following list of words: "law," "Bible," "tobacco," "wilderness," "farm," "Africa," "regal, "free," "Bannaky," "minister," "daughters," and "alone." Wood (1984) suggests a list of 14 words, but the modified list consists of 12. Typically, upper elementary students may not understand the word "regal," although they may be able to connect to a company with the word in its name, such as Regal Cinemas. If they cannot determine the category for "regal," they may choose to add it to "unknown words." As they consider the list, discussions may ensue about whether the word "*alone"* refers to a problem or an outcome. Is "wilderness*"* a setting or a problem? As students discuss and determine where each word belongs on the organizer, they are building background knowledge and starting to make meaning of the text. In small groups, pairs, or the whole class, students can build their gist statements as well as what they want to discover. During these discussions, students' critical thinking skills develop.

Text Reformulation

Text reformulation (Beers, 2003) is a by-product of story recycling (Feathers, 1993). In its original format, story recycling used a familiar text such as *Brown Bear, Brown Bear, What Do You See?* by Bill Martin Jr. (1967) as a foundation for patterned writing. In story recycling, students would take a different content area, such as U.S. presidents, and follow Martin's pattern of writing to recycle the text. For example, the recycled text may read something like "George Washington, George Washington, What do you see? I see a new nation looking at me." Students would take their knowledge about the content area and the patterned writing to reformulate the *Brown Bear* text.

In the writing strategy of text reformulation (Beers, 2003), students transform a text into another type or genre. Our example text, *Molly Bannaky* by McGill, could be reformulated into a conversation. Because students in the Intermediate stage are learning how to incorporate dialogue into their narrative writing, adding dialogue to *Molly Bannaky* would cause students to consider what conversations may sound like among the diverse characters in the historical account. Students may want to research concepts presented by McGill in order to ensure the historical accuracy of the hypothetical dialogue. The practice of text reformulation would not only develop writing skills among students but would also extend text comprehension and grammar skills.

TALL TALES

Swamp Angel by Anne Isaacs (2000) is an example tall tale text appropriate for Intermediate readers. True to the genre, *Swamp Angel* is full of irony, exaggeration, and humor. The illustrations by Paul O. Zelinsky are stunning, detailed, and consistent with the folktale period. Angel, the main character, is akin to a female Paul Bunyan, who lassoes a tornado; drinks an entire lake dry; and wrestles a menacing bear named Thundering Tarnation, who eats most of the town's food. This text is an engaging story with spectacular illustrations.

Prediction Relay

First exposure to this book could be through a read aloud, an independent read while noting story elements and exaggeration, or a prediction relay. A prediction relay is a Peer-Assisted Learning Strategy (PALS) (Fuchs et al., 2000), in which students work together in pairs. Each student acts as either "Coach" or "Player," and then they switch roles. The "Player" reads for five minutes and stops at the predetermined point to summarize the text, including details about who or what in the text, the most important part, and the main idea. If the "Player" struggles with any part of the summary, the "Coach" and the "Player" work together to summarize the reading. In addition to the traditional version of a prediction relay, students could work together to identify all the exaggerations or the story elements.

T Chart Graphic Organizer

Used as a during-reading strategy, students can identify the major elements of a tall tale (character, setting, conflict, resolution, and hyperbole) with text evidence from *Swamp Angel* by Isaacs. Readwritethink.org, a website supported by the National Council for Teachers of English (2022), has examples of T graphs along with lessons on how to use them. Another resource for tall tales is the Open Educational Resources Commons (n.d.), with specific lessons on tall tales including *Paul Bunyan, Pecos Bill, Thunder Rosa,* and *Casey Jones*. Supporting their identification of story elements with text evidence will increase their comprehension of tall tales and encourage their descriptive writing.

Write a Tall Tale

Using what they know about tall tales, a follow-up writing strategy to reading *Swamp Angel* would be to have students write their own tall tales. Tall tales usually have a regional reflection. Swamp Angel was from Tennessee, Paul Bunyan was born in Maine, and Pecos Bill was a native Texan. Students can write a regional tall tale, incorporating the story elements of character, setting, conflict, resolution, and lots of exaggeration and humor. They may want to research regional features to incorporate (e.g., Alaskan snowfalls, Florida alligators), which would add another layer of rigor to writing the tall tale. This strategy could be completed in pairs or individually, but stressing that students should have fun with the assignment by incorporating exaggeration beyond believability will engage upper elementary students in their writing.

MYTHS

The genre of myths started as oral storytelling, involving deep meaning and usually lots of symbolism. Myths also incorporate cultural factors and give meaning to elements that were unexplainable in ancient times. Typical characteristics of ancient myths incorporate traditional narrative elements of characters, setting, conflict, and resolution. In addition, myths also include metaphors, metaphorical language that analyzes a real-world event, and metamorphosis, such as demonstrating the change of a character from evil to good.

Myths have traditional story elements, but what sets myths apart from other narrative fiction genres is that characters in mythology are usually nonhuman, such as those related to a god or an animal. For example, the well-known mythological god Zeus was the god of sky and thunder, and Zeus was a main figure in Greek mythology. In addition to unique characters, myths were set in places that were familiar to the ancient culture; that is, Zeus lived on Mt. Olympus, the highest mountain in Greece. In mythology, the conflict is often a fight between good versus evil or light versus darkness, and the mythological conflict takes up a large portion of the story. However, the resolution of the mythological conflict provides a lesson to the reader/listener.

A popular mythological series for Intermediate readers is the Percy Jackson series by Rick Riordan (2005). The series has ten books and follows the journeys of Perseus "Percy" Jackson, who is a demigod son of Poseidon. In the first book, *Percy Jackson and the Olympians: The Lightning Thief*, Percy is tasked with recovering Zeus's lightning bolt. The suspected thief is Hades. The commencement of battle between good and evil begins almost immediately as Percy faces numerous mythological monsters in the Underworld. This series is engaging and captivates Intermediate readers while also expanding their basic knowledge of Greek mythology and developing their vocabulary. The example book is 680 Lexile, and all of the books in the Percy Jackson series are also written in graphic novel format.

Graphic Organizer for Note-Taking

Rick Riordan (rickriordan.com) has included many teacher guides and activity kits that correspond to his mythological books. These resources are filled with creativity and critical thinking designs. Because *Percy Jackson and the Olympians: The Lightning Thief* introduces the 12 gods of Olympus, one of the graphic organizers on the rickriordan.com site includes space for students to write facts about each god as they are presented. Using this graphic organizer for note-taking as a during-reading strategy will not only increase text comprehension but also add to the students' background knowledge about Greek mythology.

Research Writing

During the upper elementary years, students are exposed to research and learn how to use search engines to investigate facts. Since Rick Riordan already exposed readers to the 12 gods of Olympus, and students took notes in a graphic organizer on each of the gods, choosing one that they would like to know more about is a writing activity that naturally follows their reading. After they have chosen a god to learn more about, have students search the internet for additional factual information, taking notes as they read. Have students write an essay about their chosen god in a five-paragraph essay format. To help students organize their writing, many graphic organizers for writing essays are on websites such as readwritethink.org and teacherspayteachers.com.

Online Post

Many teachers have created blogs to share their expertise, but one that has multiple credentials is by Jennifer Bazzit (2020), an Intermediate teacher from Oklahoma. Bazzit's website (https://thriveingradefive.com/category/writing/) is rich with science-based learning and writing. To culminate this activity, have students post their essays online so their classmates or parents can respond. The class can vote on the strongest or their favorite god. If there are enough responses, students can even have each god win a different category.

COMICS

The genre of comics (sometimes referred to as a medium) uses images, along with text boxes or balloons, captions, and onomatopoeia, to convey the message of the story. Comic panels separate the settings and convey the sequence of the narrative. Within the genre of comics are many subgenres, including science fiction, fantasy, action/adventure, comedy, and romance. Comics are written for all levels of readers and can be an effective tool for teaching reading and writing.

Matching Texts with Comics

Comics are rife with inference. If students are not able to infer the unspoken meaning of the comic, then the message will not be understood. One way to use comics to teach inference is by printing a comic strip without the text. Students can supply text that corresponds to the illustrations to convey a message.

Another way to teach inference with comics is for the teacher to supply the text in one folder and the comic strip without text in another folder. Students must then match the appropriate text to the appropriate panel to convey the message. As students advance, teachers can have multiple comics in one folder and the corresponding texts in another folder. Students not only have to identify which text fits with the context of the comic, but then also must use context clues to identify which text fits each panel. Regardless of the comic strategy, using comics to teach inference is an engaging strategy.

It Says–I Say–and So

Making inferences may not come naturally to some students because inferences are not explicitly stated in the text. Some students, particularly struggling readers, try to keep up with literal details such as characters, setting, and events, but when they come to an inferential question, they do not know where to begin to find the answer. The after-reading strategy, It Says–I Say–And So (Beers, 2003) is a graphic organizer that helps students "see how to think" (p. 169). The chart has four columns, entitled "Question," "It Says," "I Say," and "And So." In the first column, students write the inferential question. Under the "It Says" column, students find information from the text that may help them answer the inferential question. In the "I Say" column, students think about what they know about the information in the "It Says" column. The last column, "And So," is where students combine what they know and what the text says to come up with an answer to the inferential question.

This strategy may need to be modeled and scaffolded multiple times before students are confident enough to use it independently. Modeling the strategy with a common story such as *Goldilocks and the Three Bears* may help the students understand the strategy. Reading Rockets (n.d.) (see table 5.1) illustrates this strategy using *Goldilocks and the Three Bears*.

After scaffolding this inferential strategy, students may be able to visualize what is happening in the text. Eventually students will be able to make inferences in their heads without having to fill out the graphic organizer. However, visualizing the connections between what the text says and what the student knows gives them the support they need to make the inference (Beers, 2003).

Comic Strip Creator

Having students create their own comic has multiple benefits. Kids love humor, and they enjoy telling jokes. Why not have them illustrate a comic strip using one of their jokes? Adding the visual and the dialogue to an already known joke forces students to think through the sequence of the comic as well as its inference. An interactive comic creator can help students with characters and dialogue. Multiple free comic tools are found across the internet, but a standard interactive comic creator is at readwritethink.org (https://www.readwritethink.org/classroom-resources/student-interactives/comic-creator). Some districts may have access to tools through paid subscriptions such as pixton.com. Pixton.com has multiple comic creators and corresponding teacher resources such as lesson plans and classroom comic makers.

Table 5.1 It Says–I Say–And So

Question	It Says	I Say	And So
Step 1: Write the question.	Step 2: Students find information from the text that may help answer the inferential question.	Step 3: Students write about what they know about the information in the "It Says" column.	Step 4: Students combine what they know and what the text says to come up with an answer to the inferential question.
Example Inferential Question: Why did Goldilocks break Baby Bear's chair?	The story says that Goldilocks sits in the baby chair, but she is not a baby. She is a young girl.	I say that baby chairs aren't very big. They're for babies, but Goldilocks is bigger. She weighs too much for the chair.	And so Baby Bear's chair breaks because Goldilocks is too big for it.

ADVERTISEMENTS/SOCIAL MEDIA

Advertisements and social media are filled with language that triggers emotions. Advertisements try to persuade viewers and listeners to buy a product or attend an event. Politicians use loaded language to persuade voters to adopt the POV of their campaign. Social media influencers use loaded words and visuals to inspire positive feelings. Intermediate writers are learning how to write using persuasive language.

Loaded Words

Loaded words are present in all advertisements, and fortunately for teachers, advertisements are everywhere. Loaded words are descriptive words that elicit emotion; they can be either positive or negative. Take the advertising phrase "Lose unwanted belly fat!" That phrase is filled with negative emotion. What about the grocery store advertisement that reads, "Back to School Sales Event—Find the lunches they love and the snacks that make them smile!" What parent doesn't want their kids to smile? These phrases are great illustrations of positive and negative loaded words. As a strategy, collect print or digital advertisements. Have students identify the loaded words and then organize these words as having either a positive or a negative connotation. Students can discuss the emotions that the words elicit and how the words made them feel. Persuasive words can be powerful.

Create an Advertisement

Students can apply their knowledge of the persuasive writing technique of loaded words by creating their own advertising poster or flyer. Digital applications such as Piktochart.com work well for this type of strategy and have an easy-to-use free version. In pairs or groups, have students decide what kind of products or services they are advertising. Next, they need to decide whether they are going to use positive or negative loaded words based on what emotions they want to elicit with their advertisements. After the discussion, students should create their posters or flyers incorporating their loaded words.

ANTICIPATION GUIDE REVISITED

At the beginning of the chapter, you examined four statements. Based upon what you have read in this chapter, revisit the anticipation guide statements and decide if your views are the same or have changed.

1. During the Intermediate stage, children can solve problems in a logical fashion; however, they are typically not able to think abstractly or hypothetically.
2. By the end of the Intermediate stage, readers are reading at the same rate as average adult readers.
3. Derivational suffixes change the tense or quantity of a word.
4. At the Intermediate stage of development, students are able to write an essay with a central theme using multiple sources for support.

CONCLUSION

As students master the foundational reading skills in the Transitional stage of reading, they are set up to read and write increasingly complex texts. In these years, though, because vocabulary and text become more difficult, the motivation to read and write may wane. This period has famously been called the "fourth grade slump" (Chall & Jacobs, 2003). Using motivational strategies such as peer collaboration and choice, along with engaging texts, will assist students as they progress through the Intermediate stage of literacy.

STOP AND THINK

1. Identify a text that would be appropriate for Intermediate readers. Describe the characteristics that would make it appropriate for this stage of reading development. Then describe how text reformulation could be used with this text and how this would support increased comprehension.
2. Based on the strategies described in this chapter, identify additional strategies you have discovered that you could use in your instruction for Intermediate readers and writers. Explain how and when you would use them.

REFERENCES

Bazzit, J. (2020). Thrive in grade five. https://thriveingradefive.com/category/writing/

Beers, K. (2003). *When kids can't read what teachers can do: A guide for teachers 6–12*. Heinemann.

Betts, J. (n.d.). Examples of figurative language: Guide to 12 common types. *YourDictionary*. https://examples.yourdictionary.com/examples-of-figurative-language.html

Breiseth, L. (2022). Academic language and ELLs: What teachers need to know. Colorin Colorado. https://www.colorincolorado.org/article/academic-language-and-ells-what-teachers-need-know#:~:text=While%20content%2Darea%20vocabulary%20words,words%20and%20to%20communicate%20concepts

Chall, J., & Jacobs, V. (2003). The classic study on poor children's fourth grade slump. *American Educator*, *27*(1), 14–15.

Cutting, L. E., Materek, A., Cole, C. A. S., Levine, T. M., & Mahone, E. M. (2009). Effects of fluency, oral language, and executive function on reading comprehension performance. *Annals of Dyslexia*, *59*(1), 34–54.

Dagen, A., & Bean, R. (2020). *Best practices of literacy leaders: Keys to school improvement*. Guilford.

EBSCO Connect. (2021, May 10). Lexile: Frequently asked questions. https://connect.ebsco.com/s/article/Lexiles-Frequently-Asked-Questions?language=en_US

English Language Linguistics. (n.d.). Morphological processes: Derivation versus inflection. http://www.ello.uos.de/field.php/Morphology/MorphologicalProcessesDerivationVerusInflection

Feathers, K. (1993). *Infotext*. Heinemann.

Florida Department of Education. (2022). Florida's B.E.S.T. standards English language arts. https://www.fldoe.org/core/fileparse.php/7539/urlt/elabeststandardsfinal.pdf

Fuchs, D., Fuchs, L., & Burish, P. (2000). Peer-assisted learning strategies: An evidence-based practice to promote reading achievement. *Learning Disabilities Research and Practice*, *15*(2), 85–91.

Gehsmann, K., & Templeton, S. (2022). *Teaching reading and writing: The developmental approach*. Pearson.

Gunning, T. (2020). *Creating literacy instruction for all*. Pearson.

Guthrie, J., Hoa, L., Wigfield, A., Tonks, S., Humenick, N., & Littles, E. (2007). Reading motivation and reading comprehension growth in the later elementary years. *Contemporary Educational Psychology*, *32*(3), 232–313.

Guthrie, J. T., & Klauda, S. L. (2016). Engagement and motivational processes in reading. In P. Afflerbach (Ed.), *Handbook of individual differences in reading: Reader, text, and context* (pp. 41–53). Routledge.

Isaacs, A. (2000). *Swamp angel*. Puffin Books.

Jenkins, J. R., Fuchs, L. S., van den Broek, P., Espin, C., & Deno, S. L. (2003). Sources of individual differences in reading comprehension and reading fluency. *Journal of Educational Psychology*, *95*(4), 719–729.

Martin, B. (1967). *Brown bear, brown bear, what do you see?* Henry Holt.

McGill, A. (1999). *Molly Bannaky*. HMH Books for Young Readers.

McNeill, K., & Krajcik, J. (2011). S*upporting grade 5–8 students in constructing explanations in science: The claim, evidence, and reasoning framework for talk and writing*. Pearson.

Mokhtari, K., & Niederhauser, D. (2012). Vocabulary and syntactic knowledge factors in 5th grade students' reading comprehension. *International Electronic Journal of Elementary Education*, *5*(2), 157–170.

National Council for Teachers of English. (2022). Readwritethink.org.

Open Educational Resources Commons. (n.d.). OER Commons. https://www.oercommons.org/courseware/lesson/70252/overview-old

Pearson Education. (2009). Ambiguous vowels in accented syllables. *Vowel patterns in accented syllables.* https://www.vvsd.org/cms/lib/IL01905528/Centricity/Domain/4303/sort22withkey.pdf

Piaget, J. (2000). Piaget's theory. In K. Lee (Ed.), *Childhood cognitive development: The essential readings* (pp. 33–47). Blackwell.

Read Write Think.org. (n.d.). Writing and publishing prose: Comic creator. https://www.readwritethink.org/classroom-resources/student-interactives/comic-creator

Reading Rockets. (n.d.). It says—I say—And so. https://www.readingrockets.org/pdfs/inference-graphic-organizer.pdf

Riordan, R. (n.d.). Teacher's guides. https://rickriordan.com/resource_type/teachers-guides/

Riordan, R. (2005). *Percy Jackson and the Olympians: The lightning thief.* Puffin Books.

Stahl, K. A., Flanigan, K., & McKenna, M. C. (2020). *Assessment for reading instruction.* Guilford.

Wood, K. D. (1984). Probable passages: A writing strategy. *Reading Teacher, 37*(6), 496–499.

Chapter 6

Proficient Stage

Cheri Gallman and Lin Carver

Mrs. Sutton sat in her classroom at the end of a long day grading student writing responses. She had four piles of papers in front of her, one for "exemplary" responses, a second for "proficient," a third for "showing promise," and a fourth for "not there yet." The task was based on the text *I Am Malala* (Yousafzai & Lamb, 2013). The students were initially assigned reading groups for the chapters and asked to brainstorm in an oral discussion with their groups what was meant by Malala when she wrote, "It was my grandmother's faith in my father that gave him the courage to find his own proud path he could travel along," and how she compared her relationship with her father to the relationship her father had with his father. The students were then given an independent writing assignment to explain how Malala's relationship with her mother compared to her relationship with her father.

Those who really got it recognized the differences in the values of each of her parents and used evidence to explain Malala's similarity to her father. Those who did not get it at all just made connections based on their own relationships with their parents or other adults. It was as though they had not even read the text. The sentence structure and conventions in some cases were almost nonexistent; in others there was promise.

Mrs. Sutton's pile of exemplary responses contained just two papers. The proficient pile had thoughtful responses but an abundance of sentence and grammatical errors. The "promising" and "not there yet" piles were growing by the minute; the writing was choppy, with simple sentences; it lacked both punctuation and capitalization; and the understanding of the question or the text itself was just not there. How was she going to move her "promising" and "not yet there" students to the proficient and exemplary piles? More than that, how was she going to get students who just refused to read to see the value in reading and to not become discouraged by the challenges reading presented?

How was she going to get students to think about what they were reading and not just go through the motions?

ANTICIPATION GUIDE

Read the following four statements before reading the chapter. Decide if you agree or disagree with each statement. Then read the chapter. After reading, revisit the anticipation guide and decide if your views are the same or have changed.

1. By ages 12 through 14, most students have begun developing the ability to understand symbolic ideas and abstract concepts.
2. Middle school students are focused on themselves and how their peers view them.
3. An understanding of grammar impacts writing proficiency but not reading comprehension.
4. Phonics and word analysis skills are mastered during previous stages.

MIDDLE SCHOOL: A TIME OF CHANGE

To better understand the instructional challenges Mrs. Sutton is facing in her middle school language arts classroom, it is important to have a general understanding of the middle school student. Elementary schoolers are enthusiastic about learning; high school students can often see the urgency in doing well, as their future is fast approaching; but for many middle school students, "school is an eight-hour-a-day prison that serves no higher purpose, and good luck convincing them otherwise" (We Are Teachers, 2018, para. 3). Understanding middle school students provides the foundation for developing approaches that will help our learners become more effective readers and writers. Middle school learners are unique because of where they are in their development.

If you tell someone you teach middle school, the response is often, "I'm sorry" or "You must be a saint," or the inquirer just visibly shudders. It is a time of many physical, mental, emotional, and social changes. The transition from elementary school to middle school can be a stressful, overwhelming time for children in this age group (Garrett-Hatfield, 2021).

Middle schoolers can be a little bit scary. If you consider the "insecurity, impulsivity, and hormonal imbalance [of middle schoolers] you'll find it's the rare middle schooler who doesn't occasionally victimize someone to make themselves feel better" (We Are Teachers, 2018, para. 8).

Physical Changes

Hormone levels and bodies change as puberty begins. Students may be worried about these changes and how they are viewed by others. Some middle schoolers may experience substantial drops in self-esteem as a result of these changes or experiences. While this is more prominent in females, it is seen in males as well (Garrett-Hatfield, 2021). Consequently, school tends not to be middle school students' top priority. With all that is occurring inside and outside of themselves, learning is the least of their worries!

Friends gossip and embarrass them; a social hierarchy is beginning to form; and their bodies are changing, or not changing, whether they would like them to or not. The more pressing social, emotional, and physical issues can crowd out any academic concerns (We Are Teachers, 2018). However, they are willing to learn things they consider useful and enjoy solving "real-life" problems (Pennington, 2009a, b).

Social Changes

During the middle school years, children are starting to make friends in more sophisticated ways. They are choosing friends for specific characteristics, such as shared interests, a sense of humor, and being a good person. Friends are no longer chosen just because of proximity. They are starting to realize the benefits and sometimes difficulties of friendships (NCSS, 2019). Middle schoolers will do *anything* to fit in. Somehow during this time period, it becomes not cool to be good in school, and being accepted by their peers is paramount to everything else (We Are Teachers, 2018). They tend to be self-absorbed and to exaggerate a single occurrence to be far more dire and complex than it actually is. They are sensitive and easily offended. Middle schoolers can be moody and feel alienated from people around them, but they are also curious about the world and need time to explore safely (Garrett-Hatfield, 2021).

Emotional Changes

Middle school students have already developed many social and emotional competencies (self-awareness, self-management, social awareness, relationship skills, and responsible decision-making skills) during their early childhood and elementary school experiences. They are also experiencing many developmental changes and beginning to encounter greater challenges, including increased peer and academic pressure, making these years a critical time for developing emotional skills (Schlund, 2022). Middle schoolers have intense feelings and emotions, and their moods can be unpredictable. These emotional ups and downs happen partly because they are still learning how to control and express emotions in a grown-up way. With all the changes occurring, it can be hard to get middle schoolers motivated to learn (Raising Children Network, 2022).

Middle schoolers have terrible judgment. This is where brain science becomes relevant. There is a bumper sticker that reads, "Ask your teenagers now, while they still know everything." But their judgment is based on a not yet fully developed brain. You may find that they will challenge authority figures to ascertain boundaries in an attempt to fit in while trying to understand the world around them (Garrett-Hatfield, 2021).

Cognitive Changes

Cognitively, middle school students have so much more to contribute than elementary students. By ages 12 through 14, most students have begun developing the ability to understand symbolic ideas and abstract concepts. During this period, development ranges from the concrete operational stage to the formal operational stage. Brain growth slows down during these years, resulting in more slowly expanding cognitive skills; however, these skills continue to be refined (Pennington, 2009a, b).

The Adolescent Brain

A review of the research on adolescent brain development will help build an understanding of the Proficient reader. Young adolescence is the developmental period between the ages of 10 and 15. This is the age when students develop the ability to expand their concrete knowledge to a more abstract way of thinking (Kansky, 2021). Middle school learners are developing and can hold between five to seven bits of information at a time, but teachers still need to be sure not to overwhelm them with too much information at once. Middle schoolers are quick to distance themselves from adults—including teachers—who are insincere, or who they feel do not respect their feelings and opinions. Adolescent learners benefit from moving around and hands-on experiences that allow them to draw conclusions based on data (Garrett-Hatfield, 2021).

A lot of change is happening in the brain during these years. Dr. Jay Giedd from the National Institute of Mental Health in Bethesda, Maryland, and his colleagues at McGill University in Montreal scanned the brains of 145 normal children at intervals of two years. What the researchers found is that although 95% of the brain is formed by the ages of five or six, the prefrontal cortex begins growing again just before puberty. The prefrontal cortex "acts as the CEO of the brain, controlling planning, working memory, organization, and modulating mood" (Spinks, 2000, para. 6). This area also is responsible for reasoning, impulse control, and judgments, while helping to develop empathy and self-awareness. It is one of the last parts of the brain to develop, and it can easily be impacted by hormones and emotions. Adolescents need to use the developing prefrontal cortex to analyze, reason, and make judgments as they plan and organize their responses to texts. To further complicate this ability, "the connections between the emotional part of the brain and the decision-making center are still developing—and not always at the same rate. That's why when teens have overwhelming emotional input, they can't explain later what they were thinking. They weren't thinking as much as they were feeling" (Stanford Medicine Children's Health, 2022, para. 3). Adolescent students lead with emotion, and that can be a challenge when they are asked to use logic when reading and writing.

Impact of Brain Development on Instruction

Why is this important to reading and writing in the middle grades? When students read and write, we are asking them to analyze text, show relationships, make evaluations, recognize connections, develop plans, and organize information. This happens in the prefrontal cortex, which is still developing in adolescent students. Teachers need to consider how to support this development as they plan reading and writing instruction.

Despite these challenges, for many teachers, middle school is their niche. Veteran schoolteacher of 20+ years Cheryl Mizerny, in her article "Six Reasons Why Middle School Rocks," states that teaching middle schoolers is the best job of all. Middle schoolers offer lots of variety—no day is ever the same; sometimes it is not even the same from the beginning of the class to the end. It keeps you on your toes. Middle schoolers and laughter go hand in hand; they say anything that pops into their heads, often with humorous results. Middle school students are surprisingly honest. They say exactly what they feel. They cannot keep a secret or temper their opinions. If one loves honesty, middle school is an ideal environment. Middle schoolers are quirky, curious, in a stage of discovery and finding their place in the world (Mizerny, 2015). Adolescent students can present many challenges, but this is the place where you may have a powerful impact on students' lives. They may not work hard for a grade or even a reward, but they will work hard for a teacher they like, and they will hold a teacher they care about dear long after they have left the middle school classroom.

Characteristics of Proficient Readers

Adolescent readers are motivated to read and learn, but they are impulsive. They want to learn and read about new things that are immediately useful to them (Tuychieva, 2022). Relevance is important to the adolescent reader, and they pay more attention to issues that matter to them. Adolescents are searching for themselves in what they read, and if the text is not useful to them, they often disengage (Wilkinson et al., 2020).

The adolescent tends to connect to the emotional aspects of texts. This process enables students to evaluate a complex situation from the hero's point of view in an attempt to find a moral basis for their own actions (Tuychieva, 2022).

Many teachers are familiar with the five essential reading skills: phonological awareness, phonics, fluency, vocabulary, and comprehension. However, by middle school most students will have mastered phonological awareness and the basics of phonics. Consequently, the reading skills are revised slightly to include an emphasis on word identification through morphological knowledge and a comprehension of more complex multisyllabic understandings (Iris Center, 2022).

More Complex Texts

With the integration of the Common Core came three major shifts in instruction. The first shift was that knowledge is built through content-rich nonfiction. The second was that reading, writing, and speaking are based on evidence from literary and informational text. Finally, regular practice with complex text and academic language provided the basis for literacy growth (Ready CT, 2014). When working with Proficient readers, teachers will need to devote more time when working with complex texts by providing scaffolding and strategies for reading and processing these texts as well as helping students use and access the increased amounts of domain-specific academic vocabulary.

Florida's B.E.S.T. Standards address each of these components as well. These standards are categorized into sections by subject, grade level, strand, standard, and benchmark. The strands are organized into five major sections: foundations, reading, communication, vocabulary, and ELA expectations. A teacher's job is to engage *all* students to keep trying, find evidence, problem solve, and strengthen their abilities.

Strategies for Decoding Multisyllabic Words

A simple understanding of sound-symbol relationships is not enough for success with content area texts. Middle school readers are a particularly heterogeneous group as they exhibit different patterns of reading strengths and weaknesses. Even so, about half of those who struggle with reading will benefit from instructional support in word identification, and nearly all need help with grade-level word analysis and comprehension (Iris Center, 2022).

Once phonics skills relating to letter-sound relationships are mastered in the earlier stages, students need to master the six basic syllable types and how these are combined to form multisyllabic words. A deficit at this level is evident with many struggling secondary readers, so teachers need to explore this level.

If students understand that there are six syllable types, they will be able to expand their phonics and syllabic analysis strategies (Tompkins, 2017). Teaching the six syllable types can be done by providing students an opportunity to create a poster with examples and pictures of the different syllable types. These include closed, open, "r"-controlled, vowel team, vowel silent "e," and consonant-"le" syllables. Students can create a chart or poster listing each syllable type, a picture, the sound type, and examples (see figure 6.1).

As soon as students can decode closed syllables, they are ready to start combining these closed syllables into multisyllabic words. While working on two-syllable words, this is a great time to teach students how to divide an unknown word into syllables. The only reason for doing this is so we know how many parts to pronounce in an unknown word. The goal of all phonics activities is to get the printed word into a form that is in the student's listening vocabulary. Students need to understand that each syllable only has one vowel sound.

To decode an unknown word, the student should first count the number of vowel combinations in the word. This will enable the student to determine how many syllables the word contains.

Then the student should count the number of consonants between the vowels. If there are two consonants, they typically divide between them. If there is only one consonant between the vowels, then a decision must be made. First the student should attempt to divide before the consonant, which will cause the first vowel to make the long sound. If that does not form a known word, they should divide after the vowel, which would result in the preceding syllable containing a short vowel (Carver & Pantoja, 2020).

"Phonics instruction is an important component of a comprehensive reading program . . . including structural analysis" (Carver & Pantoja, 2020, p. 65). During reading instruction, phonics and structural analysis can be used to support developing decoding skills of unknown multisyllabic words (Carver & Pantoja, 2020).

Academic Language

During the middle school years, students experience increased exposure to more complex academic language. Students must master increasingly complex vocabulary and phrases across the curriculum. Expanded vocabulary

1	Closed	Short sound cvc vc/cv	Vowel closed Cat Nap/kin Rab/bit
2	Open	Long sound v/c	Vowel open Ti/ger Fo/cus
3	r-controlled	Bossy R 1 vowel followed by r in the same syllable	Ar, er, ir, or, ur Tur/nip Car/rot
4	Vowel team	ai, ay, ee, ea, ie, ue, oa, oo, oi, oy, aw, ou	Appear in the same syllable Looking beaten
5	Vowel silent e	Long sound vce	Make flute
6	Consonant le	Consonant goes with -le at the end of the word	Bub/ble Cas/tle

Figure 6.1 Six Syllable Types

and syntactical knowledge are needed for students to achieve success across the content.

Vocabulary can be examined through a tiered approach. Beck et al. (2022) classified words into three tiers. Tier one words consist of everyday words that do not usually require instruction about their meaning. They are typically used in spoken language. Examples include "table," "home," and "baby." Tier two vocabulary are words that appear frequently across multiple content areas. These can be more challenging than tier one words since they are found more often in print than in spoken language. "Examine," "obvious," and "reflect" are examples of tier two words. Tier three vocabulary includes domain-specific words used in a particular field such as mathematics, medicine, or education. "Alliteration," "femur," and "precipitation" are examples of tier three words (Beck et al., 2022).

There are many strategies teachers can use to help Proficient readers expand their vocabulary skills. Structural analysis is an important skill that will help students understand multiple words. Students are learning about the morphological structure of words (prefixes, suffixes, and base/root words) and how these parts can be joined in various ways (Zorfass, 2014). Transitioning students' thinking from "I don't know the meaning of this word" to "What parts of this word do I recognize?" has the potential to generate a more extensive understanding of spoken and written language.

Before students read class selections, teachers need to preview and preteach vocabulary that will be important for students' comprehension of the text. They might want to provide semantic maps, graphic organizers, or "webs" that connect new vocabulary to related words and concepts when teaching new words. Teachers will also want to combine exposure and modeling with guided practice and independent, repeated oral and written application (Friedberg et al., 2017).

DISCIPLINARY LITERACY

As students move into the middle school setting, reading is often no longer a separate instructional area. During the middle school years, as students interact with more content-specific teachers, content area teachers may express frustration with their students' poor reading abilities. This occurs because students are encountering increasingly complex and sophisticated text, so the strategies they developed during earlier stages may need to be adjusted and revised (Shanahan & Shanahan, 2008).

Mastering content area subjects often requires grade-appropriate or above grade level reading skills. Consequently, educators need to know how to promote literacy skills in various content areas using before-, during-, and after-reading strategies. Strategies used by content area teachers before reading can make the difference between comprehension or a lack of comprehension. Some strategies to get students thinking about their reading include anticipation guides, KWL charts, or an SQ3R reading guide. Critical dialogues are another before-reading strategy in which conversations are centered around informational texts, videos, websites, and stories, so students can link their own experiences and knowledge to help master content knowledge in the core classes (Reutzel & Cooter, 2011).

During-reading strategies can vary depending on the content, but directed reading-thinking activity, close reading, and question-answer relationship are a few examples of during-reading strategies. After-reading strategies can include revisiting the KWL chart or working in collaborative groups to present their findings using their choice of presentation tools. "As students interact and work together with each other and their teachers to discuss the meaning of texts to improve reading comprehension, collaboration results in students obtaining great insights into the thinking process of others around a text" (Reutzel & Cooter, 2011, p. 279).

History

Reading in history class is different than reading textbooks in other content area classes. Reading a history textbook is much like reading a story, and students need to be able to identify events and people they are studying. History texts tend to be organized in chronological order using cause-and-effect relationships. These are expository texts that present the facts following a logical and objective line while attempting to limit subjective comments (Gehsmann & Templeton, 2022). Another important point to consider is that historical texts often contain analyses by the author, although aspects such as the meaning of the events; the dates, places, and other specific and immovable data; the interpretation that the author makes about them through the facts shared; and the moments analyzed within the final result are important. Students need to look at and evaluate the source of the information presented.

Regardless of the event reported, there is an introductory part in which the reader learns about the topic that will be developed. In the central part, all the information about the events is presented in a detailed, chronological, and organized manner. The author clarifies and explains the topic in depth while presenting an analysis. Finally, in the closing part the author states a concluding idea about the topic that has been developed in the course of the text (Types of Art Styles, 2021).

Science

Reading a text in science requires different skills than those in other content areas. Students need to be active readers in science, making predictions, asking questions, looking for solutions, and actively and aggressively reading the text (Croner, 2003). Scientific texts are generally presented as fact. They tend to be technical, and the information is densely packed and interconnected (Gehsmann & Templeton, 2022).

Typically, the information is presented in a hierarchical pattern of topic, subtopics, and details. Often procedural terms are used since the steps in experiments and processes need to be described. There seems to be a tendency in science, more than in other areas, to take the verb and use it as a noun. This can make the content more complex. For example, instead of saying "we demonstrated," the author may state "a demonstration was performed," resulting in a change from the active verb "demonstrated" to the noun form "demonstration" (Das, 2021).

Mathematics

Readers in a math class are required to use math-specific reading strategies or skills for decoding symbols. For students to be able to express their understanding of the math concepts, they must be able to read the content-specific vocabulary, diagrams, and examples, and understand the main features of the textbook such as the headings, index, glossary, and footnotes (Urquhart & Frazee, 2012). Reading a mathematics text is very different from reading ordinary English. Trying to read math the same way as a novel or a history text is certain to cause you trouble. In mathematics, more than any other content area, reading and rereading every word is important. Vocabulary usage is precise and exact, and even function words are important (MacAlester, n.d.). If a mathematics text asks for the "price of each box" as compared to "the price of the boxes," the answer will be very different. Students need to learn how to "unpack" a paragraph, one sentence at a time (Wong-Fillmore & Fillmore, 2012).

Reading and Evaluating Online Resources

Teaching digital literacy is a necessary component of today's middle school classrooms. It refers to the "ability to read and write using online sources and includes the ability to select sources relevant to the task, synthesize information into a coherent message, and communicate the message with an audience" (Bulger et al., 2014, p. 1568). Determining the validity of online resources can be challenging. Some online sources can be quite misleading, and students need to be able to evaluate and determine which sources are credible and which are not.

Questions to ask to determine a website's trustworthiness include the following: Does this resource list the name of its author or publisher? Is the author or publisher well known? Is the publisher one person, or is it an organization (like a museum, university, or government agency)? Is the information current? (Is there a date showing when it was written or posted?) Do other sources support this information? (Baildon & Baildon, 2012).

CHARACTERISTICS OF STRUGGLING MIDDLE SCHOOL READERS

Struggling readers tend not to question what they are reading. They do not know how to apply comprehension strategies, nor do they stop and reflect on what they have read. Struggling readers may experience difficulty recognizing vocabulary automatically and often do not read fluently. They may lack the ability to access their prior knowledge, self-monitor, make inferences, determine the author's purpose, or recognize what they enjoy reading. Secondary students who still struggle with reading often lack basic word attack ability and are not able to read unfamiliar words with accuracy (Nelson et al., 2014).

Students in Mrs. Sutton's class who were not able to successfully complete the assignment for *I Am Malala* (Yousafzai & Lamb, 2013) may not have had the foundational word attack skills necessary to read the challenging text and may have been unable to decode unfamiliar words, thus making it hard for them to read independently. Perhaps some students needed practice with fluency skills, such as accuracy, phrasing, and expression. Mrs. Sutton was disappointed that most of the students were not successful with the writing task, and she felt perhaps they did not comprehend what they were reading. To help those struggling students, Mrs. Sutton might consider including a phonics minilesson based on teacher-selected vocabulary, sentence expansion for dealing with complex sentence syntax, and building background knowledge through a fishbowl discussion.

Juicy Sentences

Embedding fun grammar lessons, such as Vocabulary Bingo and Juicy Sentence Analysis, will help those students struggling with reading smoothly and accurately. A juicy sentence is a strong sentence that is connected to the lesson, is complex, and is able to be chunked. It includes linking phrases and may contain a metaphor or simile. This strategy helps students learn to deconstruct and reconstruct sentences and to understand how different language features contribute to meaning. Using this strategy, a focused discussion on the "chunks" can take place.

Students examine the syntactical features, grammatical structures, and vocabulary in the target sentence. They can check to be sure each juicy sentence has a subject and a predicate as well as looking to be sure conjunctions are used appropriately (Student Achievement Partners, n.d.). An example sentence from *I Am Malala* (Yousafzai & Lamb, 2013) could be the following sentence: "That summer day, it was hot and sticky, and there were no windows, just a yellowed plastic sheet that flapped against the side as we bounced along Mingora's crowded rush-hour streets." The teacher writes the sentences on the board, and the class discusses the structure, vocabulary, and meaning of the sentence. Learners can then turn to their shoulder partners and discuss the syntactical features, grammatical structures, meaning, and vocabulary.

Active learning, such as having students create organizers, play word games, and discuss new or unfamiliar words, has proven to be effective in helping students retain new knowledge and increase comprehension (Reutzel & Cooter, 2011). Middle school students need to be provided with direct, explicit instruction in comprehension, vocabulary, and word recognition skills. This instruction needs to provide opportunities to actively construct meaning, practice a wide range of reading in a variety of genres and formats, increase exposure to both print and nonprint sources, develop reading as a social process for constructing meaning, and practice a wide range of comprehension strategies.

However, just because we are providing instruction for secondary readers and writers does not mean that comprehension is the only issue to be considered. Comprehension is built on many foundational skills: decoding skills, background knowledge, vocabulary, fluency, and engagement, to name just a few. All of these processes must occur simultaneously in order for readers to thoroughly comprehend the passage. All of us, including students, can only focus on one process at a time. Those students who can quickly decode, understand vocabulary, make connections, and read fluently have more cognitive energy to invest in comprehension, which is our ultimate goal (Carver & Pantoja, 2020).

Characteristics of Texts for Proficient Readers

Students in middle school will be expected to read a wider variety of texts or genres such as science fiction, biographies, fan fiction, content area nonfiction, drama, and poetry. Reading and writing processes will differ depending on genre. Engaging students in reading and writing with real-world purpose helps build excitement and should involve a variety of genres. Teachers need to teach different genre features and their functions as well as genre-specific strategies (Duke et al., 2012).

Types of Writing for Middle School

"Good writing begins with good reading" (Charron et al., 2017). Student choice in reading and writing will increase middle school learners' interest and motivation. Similar to types of reading, writing for middle school can involve a variety of formations such as expository, argumentative, or narrative writing.

Academic Writing

However, the emphasis in middle school writing tends to be on academic rather than narrative writing. This can cause the students to become less engaged, especially when they respond to prompts that are not authentic. Teachers should provide real-world writing experiences with which students can connect (Radcliffe, 2012).

Since writing is not a natural act as speaking is, writing requires direct, explicit instruction with modeling and guidance by the teacher. Our Generation Z and Generation Alpha students are never seen without their cell phones in their hands, and today's classrooms need to engage and motivate these digital natives by providing opportunities for students to collaborate online with projects that have meaning and give them a voice.

Digital Writing

Digital writing supports classroom discussion and includes more than just narrative writing (Ortlieb et al., 2016). Teachers should provide ample opportunities for writing using a variety of modalities to engage all types of learners in relevant tasks. For example, students could construct a persuasive argument for a longer lunch period or a narrative story about their hobbies. Students could choose to write in their journals, on a class blog, or in a letter.

BIOGRAPHIES AND AUTOBIOGRAPHIES

Middle school students should be exposed to biographies and autobiographies. Example texts for middle school include *I Am Malala* (Yousafzai & Lamb, 2013), *A Long Walk to Water* (Park, 2010), and *The Boy Who Harnessed the Wind* (Kamkwamba & Mealer, 2009). Depending on the reading levels of the students, these texts may be challenging and beyond their independent reading levels, so teachers may need to provide scaffolding for struggling learners. "Reading challenging texts focuses on how to bring into play the visual literacies (seeing the text), the embodied literacies (being the text), and the emotional literacies (feeling the text) while also teaching the text. It demonstrates how to layer literacies through the arts to deepen the students' connections with the challenging texts we owe them" (Fink, 2018, para. 10).

Fishbowl Discussion

A fishbowl discussion is a before-reading activity that can be used with this text. It begins with the teacher providing a few open-ended questions ahead of time, so students have time to think about the questions and prepare their responses. The class group is arranged in two concentric circles. Five or six students make up the inner circle or fishbowl and will be the ones discussing the questions, while the rest of the students will be seated around the circle listening. The job of the students in the outer circle is to listen and write down their observations. After the discussion, the students in each group reflect on what was said and write down their opinions. Students can move from being in the fishbowl to observing in the outside circle. Possible prereading questions could include the following:

1. What do you know about Malawi?
2. What does it mean to be a hero?
3. Do you need an education to be able to help your community?
4. How do people overcome adversity?

The fishbowl method encourages all students to participate and engage in active learning and holds students accountable to each other, thus building engagement and motivation in the learning process while providing the emotional security needed for working effectively with their peers.

Active learning allows students to participate in their learning rather than engage in passive learning, in which they simply receive information, to which they may or may not be listening. Strategies such as the fishbowl make learning more enjoyable, and students are more engaged and emotionally involved in their lessons (Teacher & Conklin, 2014). With adolescent learners, it is crucial for the teacher to provide collaborative or social interaction for them (Hurst et al., 2013).

Venn Diagram

After reading the story, students can reflect on their learning through writing. Students can complete a Venn diagram comparing and contrasting what they have learned about wind energy and fossil energy. Students can compare their Venn diagrams with a partner and add any additional ideas.

HISTORICAL FICTION

Historical fiction allows students to learn from the past while also being able to relate to the characters. This genre can excite and appeal to students much more than just reading their history book because they become involved with the fictional characters and can have an emotional response while reading, which provides the connections that do not occur while reading a history textbook. Through reading historical fiction, readers can relate to and learn about important historical events (Hicks & Martin, 1997). *The Watsons Go to Birmingham* (Curtis, 1995), *The Fifth of March* (Rinaldi, 1993), and *Out of the Dust* (Hesse, 1997) are a few examples of middle school historical fiction texts.

Dump and Clump

The Watsons Go to Birmingham (Curtis, 1995) is an excellent text to use for making connections by brainstorming. Dump and Clump is a prereading strategy that could be used with this text. This strategy activates prior knowledge and helps students make predictions. Students can be asked to list or "dump" all of the terms that they know relate to the topic being studied. To have them begin to identify terms, students can be asked to share any terminology they know about this period in history. Students write each term on a different Post-it note. The Post-it notes are placed on the board. After the Post-its are placed on the board, the class will "clump" similar answers together in a single square and categorize the responses by assigning labels (Scribd, n.d.). Figure 6.2 illustrates this activity.

NARRATIVE PYRAMID

For this text, students can use a narrative pyramid writing strategy to remember important details. This strategy helps students identify specific details about the story. Students draw a large six-line triangle on their paper. A specific number of words will be written on each line in the interior of the

Ideas about this Historical Period

Tone of the Era	Actions
divisive Civil unrest Tumultuous	Civil Rights Movement Campaign protests
Leaders in 1963	Social Injustice
President Kennedy Martin Luther King, Jr	discrimination segregation bullying racism

Figure 6.2 Dump and Clump

triangle. On the first line students only write one word, the name of the main character. On the second line the students provide two adjectives that describe the main character. On the third line the students provide a three-word description of the setting. This information is followed on the next line, with four words that explain the problem. The fifth line should contain five words about the events or problem in the story. The final line should contain six words about the story's solution. Because of the limited words, this activity encourages the students to express their ideas concisely.

Dystopia

Dystopian novels are set in the current or a futuristic cultural climate. For example, many dystopian novels have explored a technologically advanced society leading to personal liberties being taken away. *The Hunger Games* (Collins, 2008) is an example of a novel that appeals to teens' rebellious streak and resistance to authority. Teens often feel like they are under surveillance and can relate to the characters portrayed in these novels (Ames, 2013). *The Hunger Games* (Collins, 2008), *The Maze Runner* (Dashner, 2009), and *Ender's Game* (Card, 1972) are a few popular dystopian novels.

Personal Word List

An example of a genre-specific strategy that could be integrated into the lesson would be to ask students to discuss what they know about the themes of the story as a before-reading strategy as well as to introduce some new ideas. As students are reading, the teacher could stop at predetermined points to ask questions and discuss events in the story and have the students circle any new words from the reading, to which they would later go back and complete a vocabulary minilesson focusing on unfamiliar vocabulary. Vocabulary Bingo and creating a personal word list are two types of vocabulary activities that will build vocabulary knowledge. A personal word list helps students develop the habit of using context to determine the meaning of the word (see table 6.1) (Reutzel & Cooter, 2011).

After reading, the students could discuss the story's major theme and their views about it. As an extension activity, the students can read another text with similar themes and compare them. A graphic organizer is ideal for this, and students can later share their ideas with one another.

Concept Cubes

Personal word lists can be used effectively with concept cubes. Each pair of students is given a single cube template. The template has six sides. Students

Table 6.1 Personal Word List

New Word	What I Think It Means	Clues from the Book	Dictionary Definition
utopia			
dystopia			

will need to write one of the following directions on each of the six sides of the cube: read the vocabulary word, identify an antonym, identify a synonym, describe the category it belongs to, tell an essential characteristic, and use the word in a sentence. Then the students will tape or glue the sides to form a cube. They then roll the cube, and for the first word on their personal word list, they identify the information asked for on the side of the cube facing up. Play continues through each of the vocabulary words.

3–2–1

A 3–2–1 activity gives students a chance to summarize key ideas and identify concerns. It is an effective way to replace worksheet questions about a chapter in the text they are reading. It can be used as a quick ticket out the door activity. On a sheet of paper students list three things they found out from the chapter, two interesting things that happened, and one question they still have. Another version of this activity is that it might be changed to name three characters, identify two problems, and make one prediction. The 3–2–1 can be revised to fit any skill that is being taught.

SCIENTIFIC ARTICLES

Middle school students will be responsible for reading scientific articles and reports in various content areas. Depending on the type of academic article, the language, purpose, details, and message may vary slightly or significantly from that used in fictional texts. Students will need to have strategies in their toolbox for reading this type of information. Building background knowledge will help students understand the subject, and using narrative and digital texts on the same topic will deepen comprehension.

Adjusting Lexile Level

Sites such as Newsela, which was developed in 2013 to help students master reading and critical thinking, can be particularly effective when working with a large group of students, because the articles are written at five different Lexile levels from third grade through twelfth grade. Some of their articles are also available in Spanish, which might be helpful for second language learners (Bennett, 2020). A variety of websites are available at which articles on current topics that would be appropriate for middle school learners can be obtained. "Why Do Bees Use Social Distancing?" (Pusceddu et al., 2022) is one such article that is appropriate for Proficient readers.

Academic Language

Students will encounter unfamiliar, content-specific vocabulary while reading informational texts. Vocabulary knowledge can be divided into expressive and receptive vocabularies, which both need to be developed. The receptive vocabularies would be the words that students can understand from listening and reading. Expressive vocabularies are those words that students can understand and use correctly in their writing and speaking. According to Bean et al. (2011), preteaching vocabulary will provide the necessary background knowledge to relate the vocabulary to the text they are about to read, and reinforcing the vocabulary, after reading, will make the text more meaningful.

Using a word cloud generator as a prereading activity will expose students to the tier two and three vocabulary they will encounter in the text. To create a word cloud, the teacher copies and pastes the text into the cloud generator (https://www.freewordcloudgenerator.com/generatewordcloud). Words that are printed in larger font appear more frequently in the text. The teacher can choose the color and font that makes the clearest display for the students. In addition to the word cloud, teachers are provided with a listing of the words and their frequency (see figure 6.3).

Vocabulary Knowledge Scale

A vocabulary knowledge scale can be used as both a pre- and a post-assessment. Before discussing the vocabulary, students rate their knowledge of the word. For this text, the two new vocabulary words would be "foragers" and "immunity." Students place their responses under the column that matches their assessment of their understanding of the word: 1 = I have never seen the word, 2 = I've seen it but don't know it, 3 = I know something about this word. I think it means:, and 4 = I know this word well. I can use it in a sentence (see table 6.2).

After the lesson, students use the same form as a post-assessment of their new vocabulary knowledge. This strategy is a great way for students to self-monitor their learning. By comparing their scores on the pre- and post-vocabulary knowledge scales, they can monitor their knowledge growth.

Frequency	Word
32	bees
14	social
8	colonies
8	colony
8	bee
7	infected
7	used

Figure 6.3 Word List

Table 6.2 Vocabulary Knowledge Scale

Word	1. I've never seen this word.	2. I've seen it but don't know it.	3. I know something about this word. I think it means:	4. I know this word well. I can use it in a sentence.
foragers				
immunity				

Close Read

Close reading is a strategy used for analyzing complex text. Using a short text, students engage in multiple reads of the same text. This allows them to develop a deeper understanding of the content (Carver & Pantoja, 2020, pp. 134–135). In a close read activity, the students will read the text three times. During the first read, students will focus on key ideas and detail. For the second read, students will go back and look at craft and structure. For the third read, students will focus on what the text means to them and how it connects to other experiences (Tompkins, 2017).

A close read requires students to read with a pencil. The teacher should model how to annotate the text and provide proper scaffolding for struggling readers. This can be done with a think-aloud activity demonstrating how to predict, question, clarify, and summarize as well as code the text. Annotation, or coding the text, is where students are marking elements with consistent symbols to help with comprehension. Students are asked to annotate each page of the text as they read. At the bottom of each page, they can write a summary of relevant information drawn from their own annotations. Students can connect, visualize, comment, ask questions, predict, and summarize right on the text. This strategy is effective because students are able to reflect on how these marks aid in their comprehension. It focuses their attention on understanding what they have read.

After each reading, students can work collaboratively with each other in small groups or as partners and then come together as a class and share ideas. The teacher can then make adjustments, if needed, based on the responses from the students.

ABC Graphic Organizer

Students can create an ABC graphic organizer as a summarizing strategy after reading the article on bees and social distancing. This activity can be adjusted depending on how much time is available. Either have the students draw 26 boxes on their paper and then write one letter in each box, or if time is short, have the students write three letters in each of nine boxes. Students write one word related to the topic in each box. The word in the box must begin with one of the letters in the box. This is a fun way to review the important concepts related to the topic being studied.

Graphic Novels

Middle school students tend to be particularly interested in graphic novels. Because of the visual support, these are also a great resource to use with struggling readers who have a difficult time with decoding or comprehension. Graphic novels are content reduced and have numerous illustrations, making it easier for the reader to make sense of the text, which increases students' motivation to read (Peterson, 2010).

Providing students with a choice allows them autonomy and helps them take ownership of their learning. Since it would be hard to find one graphic novel that would interest the entire class, it would be more prudent and beneficial to allow students to choose their own books for independent reading or group reading, if other students are interested in the same text. Students can come together in literature groups to share ideas, thoughts, and opinions. They can use student discussion to share what they found interesting or important to them, what connections they made, what they found humorous, or which are their favorite parts of the text (Peterson, 2010).

Semantic Feature Map

As with any text, graphics novels can contain a variety of characters. An effective during-reading strategy is a semantic feature map. This map is a great way to compare and contrast the strengths, weaknesses, and personality traits of each of the characters. A semantic feature analysis chart or grid lists a set of concepts in the first column on the left-hand side, and each character's name is written in one column across the top. The grid is completed by placing a + sign in the box under the character's name for each character that possesses that trait. A – sign is placed in the box under the character's name if that character does not evidence that trait. This creates an easy method for comparing the characters.

Padlet

Today's digital natives are highly motivated by technology. One activity that can provide engagement is Padlet. This is an online forum in which students can write their views and feelings about the characters, and their opinions about the text. This program allows them to respond to their classmates. The teacher can start the thread by asking the students what text they selected and why. Other questions can include what they found interesting or humorous, or their favorite part and why (Padlet, n.d.). As an extension, students can create their own comic strip using a comic creator program such as Make Beliefs (https://makebeliefscomix.com/).

ANTICIPATION GUIDE REVISITED

At the beginning of the chapter, you examined four statements. Based upon what you have read in this chapter, revisit the anticipation guide statements and decide if your views are the same or have changed.

1. By ages 12 through 14, most students have begun developing the ability to understand symbolic ideas and abstract concepts.
2. Middle school students are focused on themselves and how their peers view them.
3. An understanding of grammar impacts writing proficiency but not reading comprehension.
4. Phonics and word analysis skills are mastered during previous stages.

CONCLUSION

We started this chapter by reading about Mrs. Sutton's frustration over her students' writing scores. Throughout this chapter, several instructional strategies and activities were reviewed that Mrs. Sutton could have implemented in order to foster and grow motivation and engagement as well as comprehension in her reading and writing lesson. Understanding that not all students share the same background and experience is crucial in building a successful lesson. Scaffolding and differentiating instruction is an important step in the teaching process. Some of Mrs. Sutton's students may have lacked basic word attack skills and were not able to decode unfamiliar words, thus creating a need for addressing foundational skills such as phonics, vocabulary, and fluency in the unit using a gradual release process. Motivation, socialization, and engagement are key as well, and tapping into student interests, allowing for collaboration, and making connections also would have been beneficial to the students in Mrs. Sutton's class.

STOP AND THINK

1. Understanding that middle school students focus on their peers and what they think of them, how can you use this fact in your literacy instructional practice?
2. Explain how texts at various levels can be used successfully to support learning in a middle school classroom. Identify specific texts and the variety of levels that would be used with a specific topic, and why.
3. How can you incorporate digital resources for reading and writing in the middle school classroom?

REFERENCES

Ames, M. (2013). Engaging "apolitical" adolescents: Analyzing the popularity and educational potential of dystopian literature post-9/11. *High School Journal, 97*(1), 30–20. https://doi-org.saintleo.idm.oclc.org/10.1353/hsj.2013.0023

Baildon, M., & Baildon, R. (2012). Evaluating online sources: Helping students determine trustworthiness, readability, and usefulness. *Social Studies and the Young Learner, 24*(4), 11–14. https://www.socialstudies.org/system/files/publications/articles/yl_240411.pdf

Bean, T. W., Readence, J. E., & Baldwin, R. S. (2011). *Content area literacy: An integrated approach* (10th ed.). Kendall Hunt.

Beck, I., McKeown, M., & Kucan, L. (2022). Choosing words to teach. Reading Rockets. https://www.readingrockets.org/article/choosing-words-teach

Benefield, K. (2021, September 18). Creative ABC brainstorm strategy ideas. Teaching Fourth and More! https://teachingfourth.com/abc-brainstorm-strategy/

Bennett, C. (2020). Newsela offers informational texts for all reading levels. ThoughtCo. https://www.thoughtco.com/newsela-informational-texts-all-reading-levels-4112307#:~:text=Newsela%20Reading%20Levels,at%20two%20different%20grade%20levels

Bulger, M., Mayer, R., & Metzger, M. (2014). Knowledge and processes that predict proficiency in digital literacy. *Reading & Writing, 27*(9), 1567–1583. https://doi-org.saintleo.idm.oclc.org/10.1007/s11145-014-9507-2

Card, O. S. (1972). *Ender's game*. Starscape.

Carver, L., & Pantoja, L. (2020). *Reading basics for all teachers: Supporting all learners*. Rowman & Littlefield.

Charron, N., Fenton, M., & Harris, M. (2017). *Reading with writing in mind: A guide for middle and high school educators*. Rowman & Littlefield.

Collins, S. (2008). *The hunger games*. Scholastic.

Croner, P. (2003). Strategies for teaching science content reading. *The Science Education Review, 2*(4). https://files.eric.ed.gov/fulltext/EJ1058676.pdf

Curtis, P. C. (1995). *The Watsons go to Birmingham*. Delacorte Press.

Das, N. (2021, January 7). Write science better: Avoid nominalizations. Hazlo Consultancy. https://www.hazloconsultancy.com/post/write-science-better-avoid-nominalizations#:~:text=Therefore%2C%20science%20writing%20should%20be,are%20illustrated%20in%20the%20figure

Dashner, J. (2009). *The maze runner*. Delacorte Press.

Duke, N. K., Caughlan, S., Juzwik, M. M., & Martin, N. M. (2012). Teaching genre with purpose. *Educational Leadership, 69*(6), 34–39.

Facing History and Ourselves. (n.d.). Found poems. https://www.facinghistory.org/resource-library/teaching-strategies/found-poems

Fink, L. (2018, May 24). Being challenged by challenging texts. NCTE. https://ncte.org/blog/2018/05/challenged-challenging-texts/

Friedberg, C., Mitchell, A., & Brooke, E. (2017, May 1). Understanding academic language and its connection to school success. *The Edvocate*. https://www.theedadvocate.org/academic-language-connection-school-success/

Garrett-Hatfiled, L. (2021). Traits and characteristics of middle school learners. Seattle PI. https://education.seattlepi.com/traits-characteristics-middle-school-learners-2687.html

Gehsmann, K. M., & Templeton, S. (2022). *Teaching reading and writing: The developmental approach* (2nd ed.). Pearson.

Hesse, K. (1997). *Out of the dust*. Scholastic.

Hicks, A., & Martin, D. (1997). Teaching English and history through historical fiction. *Children's Literature in Education, 28*(2), 49–59. https://doi-org.saintleo.idm.oclc.org/10.1023/A:1025067728986

Hurst, B., Wallace, R., & Nixon, S. (2013, September/October). The impact of social interaction on student learning. *Reading Horizons: A Journal of Literacy and*

Language Arts, *52*(4), 375–398. https://scholarworks.wmich.edu/cgi/viewcontent.cgi?article=3105&context=reading_horizons

Iris Center. (2022). Why do so many adolescents struggle with content-area reading? https://iris.peabody.vanderbilt.edu/module/sec-rdng2/cresource/q1/p01/

Joyce, W. B. (1999). On the free-rider problem in cooperative learning. *Journal of Education for Business*, *74*, 271–274.

Kamkwamba, W., & Mealer, B. (2009). *The boy who harnessed the wind*. Puffin Books.

Kansky, K. (2021). Leveraging the science behind the middle school brain in your teaching strategies. AMLE. https://www.amle.org/leveraging-the-science-behind-the-middle-school-brain-in-your-teaching-strategies/

MacAlester. (n.d.). How to read a math or science textbook. https://www.macalester.edu/max/wp-content/uploads/sites/120/2013/10/HowtoRead.pdf

Mizerny, C. (2015). Six reasons why middle school rocks. *Middle Web: All About the Middle Grades*. https://www.middleweb.com/24949/six-reasons-why-middle-school-rocks/

NCSS. (2022). Emotional and social development in middle childhood. National Council for the Social Studies. https://pressbooks.nscc.ca/lumenlife/chapter/emotional-and-social-development-in-middle-childhood/

Nelson, K. L., Alexander, M., Williams, N.A., & Sudweeks, R. R. (2014). Determining adolescent struggling readers' word attack skills with the core phonics survey. *Reading Improvement*, *51*(4), 333–340.

Ortlieb, E. T., Verlaan, W., Cheek, E. H., & DiMarco, D. (2016). Rethinking writing products and processes in a digital age. In *Writing instruction to support literacy success*. Emerald Group.

Padlet. (n.d.). *Padlet: You are beautiful*. https://padlet.com/

Park, L. S. (2010). *A long walk to water*. HarperCollins.

Pennington, M. (2009a, January 3). Characteristics of middle school learners. ezinearticles. https://ezinearticles.com/?Characteristics-of-Middle-School-Learners&id=1843077

Pennington, M. (2009b, January 17). Characteristics of middle school learners. *Pennington Publishing Blog*. https://blog.penningtonpublishing.com/reading/characteristics-of-middle-school-learners/

Peterson, S. (2010). Teaching with graphic novels. SCRIBD. https://www.scribd.com/book/463474051/Teaching-With-Graphic-Novels

Pusceddu, M., Cini, A., Floris, I., & Satta, A. (2022, May). Why do bees use social distancing? *Environmental Science Journal for Kids*. https://www.sciencejournalforkids.org/wp-content/uploads/2022/05/bee-distance_article.pdf

Radcliffe, B. J. (2012). Narrative as a springboard for expository and persuasive writing: James Moffett revisited. *Voices from the Middle*, *19*(3), 18–24.

Raising Children Network. (2022). Social and emotional changes in preteens and teenagers. Raising Children. https://raisingchildren.net.au/pre-teens/development/social-emotional-development/social-emotional-changes-9-15-years

Ready CT. (2014). How Common Core changes the classroom: 3 instructional shifts in ELA. https://readyct.org/2014/10/ela-shifts/

Reutzel, D. R. (2019). *Strategies for reading assessment and instruction: Helping every child succeed.* Prentice Hall.

Reutzel, R. & Cooter, R. (2011). *Strategies for reading assessment and instruction: Helping every child succeed.* Allyn & Bacon.

Rinaldi, A. (1993). *The fifth of March.* Harcourt Brace.

Schlund, J. (2022). How schools can successfully build the social and emotional competencies of middle school students. Voices in the Middle. https://safesupportivelearning.ed.gov/voices-field/how-can-schools-successfully-build-social-and-emotional-competencies-middle-school#:~:text=Middle%20schoolers%20are%20beginning%20to,group%20dynamics%20and%20resolve%20conflicts

Scribd. (n.d.). Dump and clump. https://www.scribd.com/document/418431507/Dump-and-Clump

Shanahan, T., & Shanahan, C. (2008). Teaching disciplinary literacy to adolescents: Rethinking content-area literacy. *Harvard Educational Review, 78*(1), 40–59.

Spinks, S. (2000). Adolescent brains are works in progress. In *Frontline.* https://www.pbs.org/wgbh/pages/frontline/shows/teenbrain/work/adolescent.html

Stanford Medicine Children's Health. (2022). Understanding the teen brain. https://www.stanfordchildrens.org/en/topic/default?id=understanding-the-teen-brain-1-3051

Student Achievement Partners. (n.d.). Juicy sentence guidance. Achieve the Core. https://achievethecore.org/content/upload/Juicy%20Sentence%20Guidance.pdf

Teacher, C. M., & Conklin, W. (2014). *Active learning across the content areas.* Shell Educational Publishing.

Tompkins, G. E. (2017). *Literacy for the twenty first century: A balanced approach* (7th ed.). Pearson.

Tuychdieva, M. U. (2022). Taking into account the specific characteristics of the adolescent in literary education. *Pindus Journal of Culture, Literature, and ELT, 2*(5), 249–258. http://literature.academicjournal.io/index.php/literature/article/view/381

Types of Art Styles. (2021). Historical text: What it is, main features, structure, types and more. https://typesofartstyles.com/historical-text/

University of Rochester Medical Center. (2022). Understanding the teen brain. In *Health encyclopedia.* https://www.urmc.rochester.edu/encyclopedia/content.aspx?ContentTypeID=1&ContentID=3051

Urquhart, V., & Frazee, D. (2012). *Teaching reading in the content areas if not me, then who?* ASCD.

We Are Teachers. (2018). Why teaching middle school is so hard. https://www.weareteachers.com/teaching-middle-school-is-hard/

Wilkinson, K., Andries, V., Howarth, D., Bonsall, J., Sabeti, S. L., & McGeown, S. (2020, July 22). Reading during adolescence: Why adolescents choose (or do not choose) books. *Journal of Adolescent & Adult Literacy, 64*(2), 157–166. https://doi.org/10.1002/jaal.1065

Wong-Fillmore, L., & Fillmore, C. J. (2012). *The writing workshop: Working through the hard parts (and they're all hard parts).* National Council of Teachers of English.

Yousafzai, M., & Lamb, C. (2013). *I am Malala.* Weidenfeld & Nicolson.

Zorfass, J. (2014). Word analysis to expand vocabulary development. Reading Rockets. https://www.readingrockets.org/article/word-analysis-expand-vocabulary-development

Chapter 7

Multiple Views

Lisa Ciganek

Mr. Glenn picked up his copy of *Romeo and Juliet* as fourth period began. Greeting his ninth-grade students at the door, Mr. Glenn tried to build excitement for the day's reading. "A classic love story!" he shouted to a group of girls, closely followed by, "Murder and mayhem!" to the boys right behind them. The bell rang, and Mr. Glenn prompted students to do a "turn and talk" about last night's reading of *Romeo and Juliet*, act 1. He'd sent students home with a study guide to help with the awkward Elizabethan language and questions to prompt critical thinking as they read the text independently. Circulating the room to listen for the students' reflections on the text, what Mr. Glenn heard instead were details of the previous evening's soccer game and an update on who was dating whom.

"Flat tire!" Mr. Glenn called out, signaling the end of accountable talk, and the students responded with, "Shhhhhhh!" as they quieted down. "Tell me what you think of the play so far." Silence. Mr. Glenn tried again. "Which character can you relate to at this point in the text?" It seemed as if everyone was avoiding eye contact save one student in the front row, feverishly waving his hand in the air. "Okay, how about the theme—what do you think Shakespeare is communicating about humanity and relationships?" Finally, one student piped up. "Bro, I can't even understand what they're talking about in here!" The class laughed, and Mr. Glenn sighed. The state standards required him to teach this text, but how could he get students interested in it? Mr. Glenn knew that the text would indeed be hard for some students, considering their low reading levels, but he figured that the study guide and questions would facilitate understanding. The shallow nature of student talk demonstrated that students could not process what they'd read.

Against his better judgment, but knowing the clock was ticking to the end of class, Mr. Glenn opened his book and began to explain the content of act

1. He realized he would have to come up with a better plan to engage these ninth-grade readers.

ANTICIPATION GUIDE

Read the following four statements before reading the chapter. Decide if you agree or disagree with each statement. Then read the chapter. After reading the chapter, revisit the anticipation guide and decide if your views are the same or have changed.

1. There are two types of archetypes.
2. By the time they reach high school, most students have mastered the skills they need to make meaning from their assigned texts.
3. Lexile level is the best way to determine the complexity of a text.
4. The use of strategies for supporting reading and writing can help students transform how they view themselves as readers.

HIGH SCHOOL READERS AND WRITERS

By the time students reach high school, they have engaged in reading to learn new ideas and gain knowledge from a single viewpoint (Chall, 1983). The texts they are required to read now have become increasingly complex. High school readers must evaluate multiple viewpoints as they read more widely, learning from texts across disciplines and expanding their vocabularies (Chall, 1983). Thus, an emphasis on continuing to build background knowledge is critical in the high school classroom. As we plan instruction for high school students, we should also consider the kind of readers we want them to be as they move into the postsecondary years (whether in college or career): critically thinking readers who construct and reconstruct knowledge to create their own worldviews (Chall, 1983). In this final stage of Chall's (1983) Stages of Reading Development, students display a maturity in their reading by determining how to read for their own purposes. Readers in the Construction/Reconstruction or Multiple Views stage know what portions of a text they need to read according to those purposes and can integrate new knowledge with existing understandings (Chall, 1983).

High school students who have developed both the skills and habits of reading early on typically remain stronger readers as they progress through their final years in school (vanBergen et al., 2020). By the time students reach high school, they have experienced either success or failure in reading, and those experiences shape how students engage with reading during their high school journey (Hall, 2016). Some students will openly enjoy reading and will eagerly participate in every reading assignment. Others may secretly enjoy reading but are "too cool" to admit it. Some of our readers in high school will be what Miller (2009) calls "dormant readers," students who have the capacity to read well on grade level, but do not find pleasure in reading. Required reading lists and the lack of choice in what students read contribute to their lack of interest. The average high school classroom contains advanced readers; English language learners at varying stages of language proficiency; students with disabilities; and students who are "developing readers" (Miller, 2009), still on the path to reading proficiency.

In 2019, just 34% of eighth graders in the United States performed at or above the Proficient level on the National Assessment of Educational Progress (NAEP) reading assessment (National Center for Education Statistics, 2019). Consider the classroom implications of the NAEP statistic: some of our students will enter our high school classrooms underprepared to read the rigorous literary and informational texts from which they are expected to learn. However, the challenges presented by the diverse content area texts our students are reading in high school are not necessarily indicators of whether they can read and understand complex text. In a 2005 study using American College Testing (ACT) data, less than half of high school graduates who took the ACT demonstrated readiness for college-level reading (American College Testing Service, 2006). The ACT data showed that a student's proficiency in understanding complex texts is the difference between demonstrating readiness for college and career and not being ready (American College Testing Service, 2006).

What Is a Complex Text?

The term "complex text" is often misused to describe a text as "hard." The complexity of a text is actually measured by looking at the conceptual difficulty and the linguistic challenges presented (Shanahan, n.d.). Vocabulary, sentence structure and length, figurative language, graphics, organization of information, and purpose for writing are just a few of the elements that make a text complex (Liben, 2020).

Three equally important factors make up the complexity of a text: quantitative, qualitative, and reader and text factors. All three features must be considered in measuring the complexity of a text. Quantitative measures address numerical data such as grade level bands, readability formulas (such as Flesch-Kincaid and Lexile), and leveling systems. Items such as number of syllables, word length, word frequency, and sentence length are considered. However, numbers do not tell the whole story when it comes to complexity, as is illustrated in the example provided later in the chapter (see table 7.1).

Table 7.1 Texts with Similar Quantitative Measures

Book Title	Interest Level	Publisher Recommended Grade Level Band	Lexile (Readability)	Flesh-Kincaid Reading Level (Grade)
Alexander and the Terrible, Horrible, No Good, Very Bad Day	1st–3rd grades	4.0–6.9	840L	3.5
Harry Potter and the Sorcerer's Stone	4th–8th grades	5.5–7.2	880L	8.9
The Old Man and the Sea	9th grade–adult	8.1	940L	4.0

Alexander and the Terrible, Horrible, No Good, Very Bad Day (Viorst, 1987) is a picture book typically read to first or second graders, but its Lexile score puts it in the readability band for fourth- and fifth-grade readers (MetaMetrics, 2022).

All three texts in table 7.1 have a Lexile score in the fourth- to fifth-grade range, but they are vastly different in both Flesh-Kincaid reading level and interest level.

The Old Man and the Sea (Hemingway, 1952) has traditionally been found on high school reading lists due to its content, but its Flesh-Kincaid and Lexile readabilities place it at the fourth- to fifth-grade stage. *Harry Potter and the Sorcerer's Stone* (Rowling, 1998) has inconsistencies the other way. Its interest range and Lexile score place it in the fourth-grade band, while its Flesh-Kincaid readability places it almost on the ninth-grade level. Clearly, using a quantitative measure to determine a text's complexity is not enough. Text complexity is impacted by many factors in addition to the quantitative measure of its readability.

Qualitative factors are related to content, knowledge demands, text structure, and language demands. The teacher's role in reviewing the qualitative factors of a text cannot be overstated. Teachers need to carefully examine the text and ask questions (Florida Department of Education, 2020; Liben, 2020) such as:

- What is the layout of the text? What size is the font? Are there signposts for readers?
- Are there domain-specific, academic, archaic, or ambiguous terms?
- Is the theme explicit or inferred?

- Is the organization sequential in a specific location, or does it use multiple times and places?
- Does it use figurative language or rhetoric?

Quantitative and qualitative factors impact the complexity of the text. The last and perhaps most important factor to consider when evaluating text complexity is the reader. Some questions to consider are: How do we expect the students to interact with the text? Is there specific background knowledge the students will need to possess to understand the content they are reading? Is the content appropriate for the students' age and grade level?

Establishing the complexity of a text is not a simple task. Working with colleagues teaching the same text can provide another view. Classes are composed of students with a range of abilities; there may be some texts that are complex for some learners but not others. To become Proficient readers, students need frequent practice with complex texts (Liben, 2020). It is important for students to read a variety of text types in increasing complexity across the school year.

MULTIPLE VIEW SKILL DEVELOPMENT

In their final four years of school, high school learners should continue advancing the skills formed throughout elementary and middle school. Students' continued growth can be supported through increased self-efficacy, expanded skills, and applied strategies.

Increased Self-Efficacy

We must begin our discussion of high school learners with the consideration of readers' self-efficacy. Self-efficacy is the belief in the ability to succeed in a particular situation (Bandura, 1977). Readers with self-efficacy believe they will be able to successfully perform reading tasks both now and in the future (Unrau et al., 2018). The first step to expanding students' self-efficacy is to engage them in authentic reading and writing experiences. When students believe that the work they do matters, and when they have a voice and choice in their learning, they are more likely to engage with the tasks presented to them.

Increased Relevance

Providing students with alternative ways to engage with text offers positive experiences with reading and may reshape how high school readers see themselves (Hall, 2016). Using pop-culture texts such as spoken word poetry or books adapted for movies is one such method for getting students reading and talking, because these texts relate to students' lives outside of school. Students who have had negative experiences with the kinds of texts typically used in a high school classroom may respond more positively when working with texts to which they can relate. For example, asking students to watch a video of spoken word poetry and analyzing it as a memoir engages them with a high-interest text and provides a different way for those students to demonstrate their understanding (Hall, 2016). The task becomes enjoyable for students, particularly those who struggle, and creates a positive memory related to literacy that teachers can build on as they move toward more difficult text.

Setting the expectation that all students are readers and writers communicates your belief that all students can read and write successfully. Building students' perceptions of themselves as capable readers has a positive impact on their reading comprehension (Unrau et al., 2018). Teachers play a critical role in shaping students' beliefs about themselves as readers, both with the words we speak and through the scaffolds and strategies we provide.

EXPANDED SKILLS

Throughout their high school experience, students expand their reading of literature and informational texts to include deep analyses of meaning and perspective. Teachers often take for granted that high school readers know how to think deeply about texts, make connections, and understand complicated academic language simply because they are nearing the end of their K–12 careers. Even our strongest readers still need prompting to make connections, look at text structure, and decipher syntax. A teacher's focused effort on expanded skill to scaffold comprehension through probing questions and the chance to grapple with higher-level academic language makes the difference for students (Reynolds, 2021).

MASTERING STRUCTURAL ANALYSIS

Looking back at our opening classroom vignette, Mr. Glenn mistakenly believed that simply providing students with a study guide or list of questions would be enough for them to comprehend a complex text such as *Romeo and Juliet*. For example, when teaching the advanced vocabulary word "discordant" from this play, Mr. Glenn could use a morphological scaffold such as, "What do the parts of the word tell you about its meaning?" (Reynolds, 2021). In this word, the prefix "dis" meaning "not" is used. The word ends with the suffix "ant," which means "one that performs." We are left with the Latin base word "cord," meaning "heart." This understanding could lead to learning other new words with the same base such as "accord," "concord," and "cordial."

Learning Greek and Latin roots, along with the meanings of prefixes and suffixes, helps students to enlarge their vocabularies and provides a tool with which they can discover unknown words in all academic disciplines. Familiarity with word origins also benefits students as they encounter unfamiliar vocabulary on standardized tests such as the SAT or ACT.

VOCABULARY INSTRUCTION

How should teachers decide what vocabulary to teach? A careful analysis of the texts used in the curriculum can help to discover the words that will most impact students' understanding and comprehension (Shanahan, n.d.). First, it is important to distinguish the words that will likely need to be taught directly from the words that can be learned contextually or by morphological analysis. Then, two guidelines can be used to determine the best course of action for vocabulary instruction. (Fisher, et al., 2016; Shanahan, n.d.).

If the word is related to a concept students will know, and it will be required for text-related tasks (reading, writing, discussion), and it appears repeatedly in the text, and neither contextual nor structural analysis leads to meaning, then teach the word to students. On the other hand, if the word is related to a concept students will know, and it will be required for text-related tasks (reading, writing, discussion), and it appears students could use either contextual or structural analysis to discover the word's meaning (with or without prompting), then it is not necessary to preteach the word.

Vocabulary development is not limited to academic, domain-specific words. As students move into reading more complex texts, they are exposed to foreign words and phrases commonly used in English (*carpe diem, faux pas, coup de grâce*).

NEW SKILLS

Fluent writers have a natural rhythm and flow in their writing; they use grade-appropriate vocabulary and elaborative techniques. The current age of digital communication, in which students "write" in characters and emojis, makes the time needed to write a literary analysis, essay, or report seem unappealing—and frustrating—to some students. Chunking longer writing assignments into smaller pieces, using graphic organizers, and teaching minilessons on key elements of the writer's craft are effective methods for scaffolding writers.

Additional Figurative Language

Another way to scaffold Mr. Glenn's learners would be to teach essential figurative language. Personification, alliteration, idioms, similes, and metaphors have been taught in earlier stages of reading and writing, so these may only need to be reviewed. However, during the high school years, students are just being exposed to allusions, hyperbole, imagery, meiosis, satire, and onomatopoeia. Many classical works of prose and poetry contain figurative language that points to deeper meanings and creates a mood.

In the middle school level, students developed an understanding of stereotypes. A stereotype is when the image of a person, group, tribe, or region is characterized through generalizations. Students may have been exposed to novels that use explicit stereotyping, in which a specific person or group is presented using broad generalizations. In some cases, the stereotyping becomes a weapon to stigmatize an individual or group. Stereotyping can also be implicit because the victims are not aware of the stereotyping and have no control of their being victims. *The Book Thief* (Zusak, 2005) is an example of stereotyping the Nazis (Literary Devices, 2022b).

Archetypes

High school readers build on this concept of stereotyping to develop an understanding of three types of archetypes: character archetypes, situational archetypes, and symbolic archetypes. This knowledge can help to scaffold readers as they encounter complex literary text. An archetype is a literary device, based on the work of Carl Jung, in which a character is created with a typical set of qualities or traits. In the literary context, archetypes are characters, images, or themes that embody universal meaning and experiences. The hero is one of the most common literary archetypes, although there are twelve primary character archetypes.

- Lover: individual guided by emotion and passion
- Hero: protagonist who rises to a challenge
- Outlaw: rebellious individual outside societal conventions
- Magician: powerful individual who uses universal forces
- Explorer: individual driven to explore the unknown
- Sage: wise and knowledgeable individual
- Creator: individual who creates something significant
- Innocent: "pure" character in terms of morality or intentions

- Caregiver: individual who often sacrifices for others
- Jester: individual with humor and comic relief
- Everyman: average, relatable character found in everyday life
- Ruler: individual with legal or emotional power or control over others

Mr. Glenn could scaffold his students' understanding of the play by teaching his students about character archetypes. He might want to begin this discussion using movie characters. Then he could ask small groups of students to provide a second example for each archetype (Jeter & Kash, 2022). Building on this knowledge, students could extend their learning to *Romeo and Juliet*. In this play, Romeo and Juliet are the lovers, Friar Laurence is the sage, and Mercutio is the caregiver (Literary Devices, 2022a).

The same process could be used for teaching about situational archetypes (good vs. evil, magic weapon, rags to riches, etc.). Tolkien's *The Lord of the Rings* (1954) is an example of a situational archetype, while the *Lord of the Flies* (Golding, 1954) is an example of a setting archetype. Setting archetypes would be used to convey the emotions and ideas associated with a particular setting, such as the garden, the island, or the small town. The last type of archetype is the symbolic archetypes. These include colors, shapes, and natural events (water, fire) (YourDictionary, 2022).

Developing Arguments

As learners progress through the high school years, they are being asked to evaluate more extensively their own and others' reasoning. They are developing an understanding that an argument can be constructed to be inductive, deductive, or causal. An inductive argument moves from sufficient, typical, and representative examples to the conclusion, while deductive reasoning builds from the known specifics to the conclusion. The causal argument establishes a relationship between the cause and an effect.

When developing a persuasive argument, high schoolers are learning to use the three types of rhetoric: ethos, pathos, and logos. Ethos involves the speaker or writer using their reputation, virtue, intelligence, or personal qualities to convince others. When using pathos, the speaker or writer uses emotional appeals to cause individuals to experience an emotion such as empathy, desire, or anger. When using logos, the speaker or writer focuses on showing the rational validity of the argument through facts, data, or statistics (Kalama, 2020).

Fallacies in Arguments

When evaluating an argument, it is important to be able to recognize the fallacies in the argument. There are ten that are the most common. These include hasty generalizations, false analogies, false causes, false authorities, bandwagon, false dilemmas, ad hominem, slippery slopes, red herrings, and appeals to tradition. Knowing how to identify types of reasoning and fallacies in reasoning helps readers to evaluate arguments in literature and informational text. High school learners will be eligible to vote during or just after their twelfth-grade year, so possessing this evaluative skill can be applied almost immediately to politics and life outside of the school setting (University of Minnesota, 2022).

WRITTEN STRUCTURE AND SYNTAX SKILLS

Like reading, some teachers may not realize the need for teaching writing to high schoolers; instead these teachers are merely assigning and grading writing tasks. There is a difference! High school learners should continue actively learning appropriate writing structures and syntax as they write for authentic purposes. High school writers extend their writing skills in three main areas: narrative, argumentative, and expository. Effective high school educators consistently review and reinforce writing conventions as they teach students to refine their writing using parallel structure; applying standard grammatical agreement; and varying phrases, clauses, and sentence structure.

Active versus Passive Voice

High school students are learning how, when, and why to use active or passive voice. In the active voice, the subject of the sentence is performing the action, while in the passive voice the sentence is switched so that the subject is being acted upon by the verb. The tone of a sentence written in active voice is direct and clear and focuses the reader's attention on the subject of the sentence. Active voice is typically used for most nonscientific writing.

If instead the reader's focus should be on the action rather than the subject, the passive tone would be the more appropriate choice (Kramer, 2022). One simple way to help students understand active and passive voice is to have them identify it in written texts. Teachers might consider using a popular piece of fiction or a text that students are required to read. They might ask students to highlight active voice in one color and passive voice in another. When focusing on active and passive voice in student writing, educators might provide a selection of photos (or ask students to supply a picture that is meaningful to them) and have students write about the picture first in the passive voice, then rewrite the same information in the active voice, noting the differences.

Grammatical Structures

Students are expected to have mastered most grammatical constructions by the end of their middle school years. During high school instruction, students are expected to review and master the appropriate use of semicolons, ellipses, colons, and hyphens. By the end of their high school career, they should be able to appropriately implement usage rules to express their ideas smoothly, clearly, and logically in oral and written formats.

As we plan reading and writing instruction for our high school learners, it is critical to think purposefully about what scaffolds are needed for their success. Educators need to preview the text to be taught and to consider its complexity. What background knowledge do students need to possess to interact successfully with the text? What kinds of minilessons will readers need to reach the intended learning target? What supports will students need to overcome the roadblocks they may encounter on their way to that reading or writing learning target? What type of feedback strategies will move them toward reading or writing proficiency in this grade level and beyond? (Tovani, 2021).

Genre Reading and Writing Strategies

High school students need experience with reading and writing in ways that are meaningful to them. The rise in youth social activism demands that teachers give students a chance to use their skills for purposeful action in their communities (Burns et al., 2019). Whether preparing for college or career, high school students need strong comprehension, vocabulary, and fluency skills. Comprehending the complex texts students will encounter in high school and beyond, then expressing their understanding about those texts, requires students to have a toolbox of reading and writing strategies. The same is true for our students entering skilled trades, where there are complex instructional and policy manuals involving high-level vocabulary and sentence structure (Wexler, 2022). Core skills for success include reading complex texts independently and strategically, reading closely, synthesizing ideas across texts, and focusing on a reading task over an extended period (Springer et al., 2014). Because the prefrontal cortex (the place of executive function) does not fully develop until students are in their early twenties, students may struggle with those core skills (Medina, 2018). Teaching and modeling active reading strategies will help students, because when they are actively trying to understand what they read, they comprehend more (Shanahan, n.d.).

Many high-quality strategies exist for developing comprehension and fluent writing in our high school learners. Using a gradual release of responsibility framework, teachers should provide direct instruction on each strategy, model its use during guided practice, engage students in collaborative learning with peers to extend their understanding of the strategy, and allow for internalization of the strategy through independent practice and multiple exposures (Fisher & Frey, 2022). It is important that students understand not just how to use the strategy but also when and why it is beneficial. Teaching some of the strategies we use in our own personal reading connects us with our readers and helps them see the value of learning each strategy. Throughout the remainder of this section, reading and writing strategies for a variety of text types used in high school classrooms are discussed.

DRAMA

When reading a complex text such as *Romeo and Juliet*, students would benefit from having a way to track their thinking across the multiple acts with an ever-growing list of characters. As Mr. Glenn discovered in our opening classroom vignette, readers are less likely to read difficult text without specific strategies to assist them in making meaning from the text. True, Mr. Glenn did provide a study guide and questions, but students did not find the materials useful in helping them think critically about the play. Character double-entry journals (Tovani, 2021) present students with a way to capture their thinking over time as they continually revisit a text. The structure is simple: the reader lists evidence about the character from the text on the left side of the paper and uses the right side of the page to communicate their thinking. Students learn to monitor their own understanding throughout a text and, in a way, talk back to the text.

Character Double-Entry Journal

When using double-entry journals, students identify areas of confusion, make connections and inferences, ask questions, share new thinking, and engage in other forms of self-monitoring behavior. Mr. Glenn could model the use of a double-entry character journal with his readers utilizing a simpler text and prompts (such as "As I read this part, I'm thinking . . . " or "I'm wondering about . . . ") and then move into its use with *Romeo and Juliet* as guided practice. For example, Mr. Glenn's students can use a double-entry journal to think about the characters as they prepare for discussion and a character analysis activity (see table 7.2).

Multiple Views 139

Table 7.2 Character Double-Entry Journal

Line(s) from act 1 that tells me something about the characters	What this part of the text tells me about the character(s) or Something I'm wondering about the character(s)
Tybalt (scene 1, lines 65–67) What, drawn and talk of peace! I hate the word, As I hate hell, all Montagues, and thee. Have at thee, coward!	Tybalt really hates the Montagues. He hates the person he's talking to. He's a fighter!
Romeo (scene 4, lines 9–10 and 12–14) Give me a torch; I am not for this ambling. Being but heavy, I will bear the light. Not I, believe me. You have dancing shoes With nimble soles. I have a soul of lead So stakes me to the ground I cannot move.	Romeo is upset. I think it's because he's not feeling the love from Rosaline.

Character double-entry journals offer teachers a view into students' thinking, thus serving as an informal assessment. Mr. Glenn could easily determine from a review of the students' journals any concepts that need reteaching or clarification. He could also use the journals to plan additional strategy instruction for small groups or enrichment opportunities for students demonstrating advanced thinking. Once the use of double-entry journals is internalized, high school readers may find this strategy to be valuable across other content areas.

Character Résumé

Character double-entry journals can also serve as scaffolds for students during discussions and as a means for preparing to transfer their thoughts to a writing piece. As we have learned, high school students enjoy learning in ways that are authentic to their lives. Instead of asking them to write yet another essay, consider writing assignments that allow for creativity and cultural relevance while delivering practice for needed soft employability skills such as clear communication and organizing ideas. A character résumé is one approach to writing with *Romeo and Juliet*.

Teaching students to write a character's résumé provides an excellent opportunity to collaborate with educational colleagues. The business teacher, career coach, or guidance counselor could partner with the instructor to teach students appropriate résumé formatting. Again, character résumé writing affords flexibility in content and structure. Students might want to consider including details such as the character's personal traits, revealing quotes from the character, strengths and weaknesses, references (Which character would vouch for this one?) and experience (the character's role in the development of the story). Alternatives to character résumé writing could be LinkedIn or Instagram profiles.

SPEECHES

"The Danger of a Single Story" (Adichie, 2009) was originally presented as a TED talk and remains a culturally relevant piece for analysis. Teachers have options for presenting the speech to students depending on the learners in their classrooms. Students could read the speech transcript first, discuss it, and then watch the TED talk video, or vice versa. Another alternative would be to distribute the transcript just before watching the video for the first time so that students could see and hear the content simultaneously.

Student-Constructed Concept Map

A concept map is a graphic organizer that high school readers can use to consider the "big ideas" in the speech and make personal connections as they negotiate meaning from the text. It is an effective tool for student thinking both before and after reading. There are various ways to engage students in using concept maps, but a key element in their use is that students should generate their own maps as they process the speech rather than copy a teacher-created map (Fisher & Frey, 2020).

This activity could begin by having the teacher identify a topic or ask a question related to the text, then students can brainstorm words and phrases they associate with the topic. For example, when teaching with Adichie's (2009) speech, prejudice or stereotype might be topics to explore ("Stereotypes and 'Single Stories,'" n.d.). Students can suggest related words and phrases. Then they can sort and categorize their ideas, organizing them visually in ways that show the students' understandings and their connections with the main topic. By drawing lines, arrows, or other symbols, they can show the relationships between their ideas and the topic. Finally, students can write a short explanation that describes their connections or create a key to the organizer (see figure 7.1).

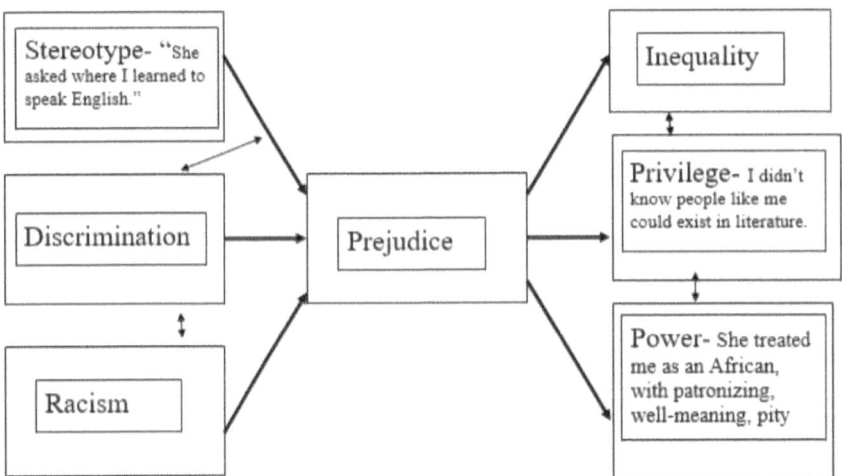

Figure 7.1 "Danger of a Single Story" Concept Map

It will increase student engagement if educators provide an opportunity for students to share and discuss their maps with peers, either through a turn and talk or in small groups. The rich discussion will expand students' perspectives and may result in the addition of ideas to their concept maps. The students should keep the maps at hand as they read and/or listen to the speech so they can add new ideas or quotes.

RAFT

Concept maps and other graphic organizers are often seen as a product of learning rather than a tool for learning. Once students have created and elaborated their concept maps, they can use them as a means for responding to the speech. RAFT writing (Vacca et al., 2011) is a strategy for students to consider other perspectives on a topic and respond to complex text, allowing them to engage in critical thinking and demonstrate their understanding. The acronym RAFT stands for role, audience, format, and topic; each of these may be assigned by the teacher or self-selected by students.

To use the RAFT framework, students adopt a particular role as the writer, for example, a historian, journalist, or citizen. They write to a specific audience, such as a committee, the government, or the public. The format of the writing could be a letter, an editorial, or a tweet. The topic will relate directly to the text being read, in this case, a speech about prejudice. When we first introduce RAFT writing to students, it helps for everyone to write in the same role and format, on the same topic, to the same audience. As students become more comfortable with the structure and develop in their ability to deal with multiple perspectives, we can assign multiple roles and audiences to groups within the class and encourage students to choose their own formats. Students can also self-select roles, audiences, and formats from a list of options. RAFT writing connects with student learning in the content areas and is an excellent tool for differentiation.

Text Structure

Learners will be exposed to a variety of text types throughout high school. When students recognize the structure of a text as they read, they are more likely to comprehend the material (Hebert et al., 2016). Text structure is the way authors organize information to convey meaning and achieve their purposes for writing. We can compare text structure to a building: when you walk into a hospital, for example, the structure of the hallways, doors, and rooms helps visitors navigate the building. Similarly, the way a text is structured gives the reader clues for navigating meaning. Common text structures include problem/solution, cause/effect, description, chronological, and compare/contrast. Struggling readers, students with disabilities, and English language learners in particular benefit from instruction in text structure (Shanahan, 2021).

Blogs

Blogs are one form of informational text that high school learners can use to practice identifying text structure. A blog is a type of digital journal. Posts appear chronologically, with the most recent entry at the top, or posts may also be sorted by topic or keyword. Blog posts are engaging for introducing text structure because the content is interesting, and the posts are typically short and not overly complex. Posts from a high-interest, current website such as College Info Geek (www.collegeinfogeek.com) will prove beneficial. This site houses a collection of articles on studying, preparing for college, developing good financial habits, and so on. Thomas Frank's (2017) post entitled "How to Make Studying Fun" should pique your high school learners' curiosity.

As with every strategy, be explicit in teaching text structure to students. Teach one structure at a time and explain that analyzing how a text is structured will help students to gain meaning from it. Encourage students to read a text through once before trying to analyze its structure. Use a think-aloud approach as you move through the blog post together so students can see and hear how you are discovering the text structure. Point out transition or connective words that provide clues to the type of structure being used. It may help to construct anchor charts for each type of text structure as you teach it so students can refer to the chart when reading or writing.

Text Scavenger Hunt

Once students have grasped a particular text structure in reading, have students use that text structure in their writing. Start small with this; model paragraph writing using a particular structure, then release students to try the same. As students become more proficient, have them write a paragraph and exchange it with a peer to see if their classmates can identify the text structure being used. Giving students the chance to write their own blog posts using one of the learned text structures will build excitement and increase student buy-in for writing.

The brief paragraphs the students have written can be used to reinforce this skill. For this activity, divide the class into small groups. Give each group five to six passages and have them place a number on each passage. On a sheet of paper one member of the group should record the text structure that the group has agreed on for that passage. The first group to identify all their passages correctly is the winning group.

ARGUMENTATIVE TEXT

How many times have you read an article or a book chapter, come to the end, and wondered, "What did I just read?" Our high school students may experience this regularly with the informational texts they are required to read. Teaching learners to annotate while reading helps them to interact with the text and read with purpose. Most students will tell you they already highlight text, but we need to help them understand that annotating is different and will contribute to a much deeper understanding of the material.

Annotation

Annotation is a valuable tool for deciphering complex text. When reading an editorial such as "To the Public" (Garrison, 1831), students will undoubtedly have questions about the vocabulary, the context, and the content of the piece. Written by abolitionist William Lloyd Garrison, the editorial was a bold statement on slavery and contains much more formal language than some of the more contemporary texts students are reading. Asking students to jot down their thinking right in the text as they read will draw on their "inner voice" (Tovani, 2021) as they talk back to the author and the text. Teacher modeling of this strategy is critical; otherwise students will tell you that they were not thinking anything or did not have any questions.

Annotating is a flexible strategy; when you first introduce it, you may wish to specify the kinds of annotations students should make: connections, inferences, questions, and so on. Annotations can take many forms; they can include words or phrases, definitions, underlining, circling, paraphrasing, notes in the margin, and illustrations. Ensure that students have a copy of the text on which they can write and give them wide margins for writing their thinking. Collaborative annotations, done in small peer groups, allow for shared thinking and discussion of a common text. The teacher may want students to annotate for a specific purpose, such as annotating all the evidence that points to the central idea. Once annotating becomes second nature, students can use annotations more purposefully and more personally based on their reading needs. Observe the annotations used in the excerpt of "To the Public" in figure 7.2.

"To the Public" is an argumentative piece. Students need to understand that argumentative writing is not solely an expression of someone's opinion or viewpoint. They should be able to identify the claim and the evidence, and

---

He agrees with this passage in the Declaration of Independence)

Assenting to the "self-evident truth" maintained in the American Declaration of Independence, "that all men are created equal, and endowed by their Creator with certain inalienable rights – among which are life, liberty, and the pursuit of happiness," I shall strenuously contend for the immediate enfranchisement of our slave population. In Park-Street Church, on the Fourth of July, 1829, in an address on slavery, I unreflectingly assented to the popular but pernicious doctrine of gradual abolition. I seize this opportunity to make a full and unequivocal recantation, and thus publicly to ask pardon of my God, of my country, and of my brethren the poor slaves, for having uttered a sentiment so full of timidity, injustice, and absurdity.

Key: Underline the central idea. Circle words you still need to know the meaning of. Box your thinking in the margins.

Figure 7.2 "To the Public" Annotation

consider potential counterclaims to the argument. It can be helpful to teach students to look for phrases such as, "On the other hand . . . " or "This is not to say that . . . " (Graff & Birkenstein, 2021) that provide clues while they are reading and when they write their own arguments. The op-eds in your local newspaper or from The New York Times Learning Network are additional sources of argumentative text.

Backwards Outlining

Backwards outlining (Facing History and Ourselves, 2021) functions as a tool for both reading and writing with Garrison's (1831) editorial. Designed as a strategy for peers to give feedback on each other's writing, backwards outlining can be used simultaneously to help students extract meaning from a text and to facilitate summary writing. This is a strategy students can use independently because they should already know how to create an outline. Once students have read and annotated "To the Public," have them create an outline for the text. Ask them to include the thesis or claim, arguments, and evidence. Then students can pair up and compare their outlines. Did their partner pull out additional evidence or view the argument through a different lens? Using their refined outlines, students could write a summary of the argumentative piece. Student pairs can exchange summaries and engage in the backwards outline process one more time to provide feedback on the writing. Learners would look for any critical elements missing from the summary. Outlines can also be used as a form of assessment.

POETRY

If Mr. Glenn were to mention poetry in his ninth-grade classroom, he would likely hear a collective groan from his students. Poetry is rich in language, but the mysteries of a poem's meaning remain elusive to high school students. An easy and engaging way to gain student buy-in for studying poetry is to use song lyrics. Ask students to bring in the lyrics of their favorite songs (school appropriate, of course). Allow students to work collaboratively on discovering the meaning behind their songs. Encourage them to ask questions: Why did the songwriter choose this phrase? How is the songwriter feeling? Why did the songwriter repeat this part multiple times? Asking questions such as these will lead into the use of Questioning the Author (Beck et al., 1997; Beck et al., 2020).

Questioning the Author

Questioning the Author (QtA) is a strategy used during reading to support students as they strive to make meaning from the text. The goal is for students to think critically and move past literal interpretations. QtA is a strategy that requires preparation on the teacher's part: reading the text and monitoring your own comprehension, finding appropriate stopping points for discussion, and writing probing questions. It is important to consider the key elements about which you want students to make meaning. Try it with this excerpt from Robert Frost's (1914) "Mending Wall":

> He is all pine, and I am apple orchard.
> My apple trees will never get across
> And eat the cones under his pines, I tell him.
> He only says, "Good fences make good neighbors."
> Spring is the mischief in me, and I wonder
> If I could put a notion in his head:
> "Why do they make good neighbors? Isn't it
> Where there are cows?" But here there are no cows.
> Before I built a wall, I'd ask to know
> What I was walling in or walling out,
> And to whom I was like to give offense.

As they prepare, teachers should ask themselves questions such as these: What are the major points of this section? What possible challenges will students have with this portion of the text? How did I make meaning in this section? Where are the natural stopping points for discussion?

The next step is to create probing questions that will provoke deep student thinking with the text as they read it and stop at the predetermined points. Students will need to be led to understand that the objective is not to come up with a "right" answer, but instead to be comfortable wrestling with the text and wondering about the author's thinking and purpose (Beck et al., 1997; Beck et al., 2020). The questions are not meant to gauge student understanding of the text, but to facilitate their construction of meaning. Beck et al. (1997) outlined three types of questions for discussion: initiating prompts, follow-up prompts, and narrative prompts. Initiating prompts are questions such as, "What is the author trying to say?" and "What is the author's message?" Follow-up prompts require the students to think critically about what the author has already written and ask questions like, "Does this make sense with what the author told us already?" Follow-up prompts can also point to within-text relationships such as, "How does this connect with what the author told us in the _____ section?" Last, students can be encouraged to ask questions in narrative text with prompts like, "Given what you know about this character, what do you think he will do next?"

It is important to note that the question prompts are not designed for teacher–student–teacher interaction, but rather to foster discussion among the students as they construct ideas. The teacher can rephrase what a student says, respond with another question, turn the students back to the text, fill in gaps in the construction of meaning, and recap what was said (Beck et al., 1997) to keep the conversation flowing and ensure the major concepts are discussed.

Original Poems

As students write their own poems, use QtA in student pairs to provide additional practice in the construction of meaning and engage students in giving feedback on each other's writing.

ANTICIPATION GUIDE REVISITED

At the beginning of the chapter, you examined four statements. Based upon what you have read in this chapter, revisit the anticipation guide statements and decide if your views are the same or have changed.

1. There are two types of archetypes.
2. By the time they reach high school, most students have mastered the skills they need to make meaning from their assigned texts.
3. Lexile level is the best way to determine the complexity of a text.
4. The use of strategies for supporting reading and writing can help students transform how they view themselves as readers.

CONCLUSION

We began this chapter observing Mr. Glenn as he engaged with ninth-grade readers during his fourth period class. Mr. Glenn will find that integrating reading and writing activities before, during, and after a challenging text such as *Romeo and Juliet* deepens his readers' understanding. When he provides students with targeted strategies to help them hold their thinking, followed by meaningful, authentic writing opportunities, Mr. Glenn will cultivate the kinds of readers and writers who are well prepared for the rigors of literacy in college and career.

STOP AND THINK

1. Work with a colleague to evaluate the complexity of a text you are reading or teaching with.
2. Why do scaffolds, strategies, and self-efficacy matter for high school readers and writers?
3. Choose one of the strategies from this chapter. Try it with a high school text of your choice. How would you explain the strategy to your students? Are there ways you would need to scaffold the strategy for your learners?
4. What are additional strategies you have discovered that you could use in your instruction for high school readers and writers? Explain how and when you would use them.

REFERENCES

Adichie, C. (2009). The danger of a single story [Speech audio recording]. https://www.ted.com/talks/chimamanda_ngozi_adichie_the_danger_of_a_single_story

American College Testing Service. (2006). *Reading between the lines: What the ACT reveals about college readiness in reading*. ERIC. https://files.eric.ed.gov/fulltext/ED490828.pdf

Bandura, A. (1977). Self-efficacy: Toward a unifying theory of behavioral change. *Psychological Review*, *84*(2), 191–215.

Beck, I., McKeown, M., & Sandora, C. (2020). *Robust comprehension instruction with questioning the author: Fifteen years smarter*. Guilford Press.

Beck, I. L., McKeown, M. G., Hamilton, R. L., & Kucan, L. (1997). *Questioning the author: An approach for enhancing student engagement with text*. International Reading Association.

Burns, L. D., Faris, A., Melino, F., Turner, W., & Wheatley, A. (2019). Creating conditions for literate engagement: Teaching, learning, and acting in the world. *Journal of Adolescent & Adult Literacy*, *63*(2), 201–208. http://doi.org/10.1002/jaal.981

Chall, J. S. (1983). *Stages of reading development*. McGraw-Hill.

Facing History and Ourselves. (2021). Writing strategies. https://www.facinghistory.org/sites/default/files/Argumentative_Writing_Strategies.pdf

Fisher, D., & Frey, N. (2018). *Improving adolescent literacy: Content area strategies at work*. Pearson.

Fisher, D., & Frey, N. (2022). Past successes, new ideas. *Literacy Today*, *40*(1), 26–29.

Fisher, D., Frey, N., & Hattie, J. (2016). *Visible learning for literacy, grades K–12: Implementing the practices that work best to accelerate student learning*. Corwin Literacy.

Florida Department of Education. (2020). *Florida's B.E.S.T. standards: English language arts.* https://www.fldoe.org/core/fileparse.php/7539/urlt/elabeststandardsfinal.pdf

Frank, T. (2017, September 19). How to make studying fun. College Info Geek. https://collegeinfogeek.com/how-to-make-studying-fun/

Frost, R. (1914). *Mending wall.* Poets.org. https://poets.org/poem/mending-wall

Garrison, W. L. (1831, January 1). To the public. *The Liberator.* https://www.pbs.org/wgbh/aia/part4/4h2928t.html

Golding, W. (1954). *Lord of the flies.* Faber & Faber.

Graff, G., & Birkenstein, C. (2021). *They say, I say: The moves that matter in academic writing.* W. W. Norton.

Hall, L. (2016). Reconfiguring the reading experience: Using pop culture texts to shift reading narratives. *Journal of Adolescent & Adult Literacy, 60*(3), 341–344. http://doi.org/10.1002/Njaoavle.5m94b

Hebert, M., Bohaty, J. J., Nelson, J. R., & Brown, J. (2016). The effects of text structure instruction on expository reading comprehension: A meta-analysis. *Journal of Educational Psychology, 108,* 609. http://doi.org/ 10.1037/edu0000082

Hemingway, E. (1952). *The old man and the sea.* Simon & Schuster.

Jeter, G., & Kash, S. (2022, May 16). Locating archetypes in pop culture, literature, and life. *Authentic Lessons for 21st Century Learning.* https://learn.k20center.ou.edu/lesson/383

Kalama, W. (2020, December 3). Ethos, pathos, logos: What are they and how to use them. *Words Matter.* https://www.wix.com/wordsmatter/blog/2020/12/ethos-pathos-logos/

Kramer, L. (2022, April 20). Active vs. passive voice. Grammarly. https://www.grammarly.com/blog/active-vs-passive-voice/

Liben, D. (2020). Text complexity. In J. Patterson (Ed.), *In the SAT® suite and classroom practice: English language arts* (pp. 9–29). College Board.

Literary Devices. (2022a). Archetypes. https://literarydevices.net/archetype/

Literary Devices. (2022b). Stereotypes. https://literarydevices.net/stereotype/

Medina, J. (2018). *Attack of the teenage brain: Understanding and supporting the weird and wonderful adolescent learner.* ASCD.

MetaMetrics. (2022). Measuring growth with Lexile measures: College and career readiness. Lexile: Framework for Reading. https://lexile.com/educators/measuring-growth-with-lexile/college-and-career-readiness/

Miller, D. (2009). *The book whisperer: Awakening the inner reader in every child.* Jossey-Bass.

National Center for Education Statistics. (2019). *National Assessment of Educational Progress: The nation's report card.* https://nces.ed.gov/nationsreportcard/reading/achieve.aspx

New York Times. (n.d.). The Learning Network. https://www.nytimes.com/section/learning

Reynolds, D. (2021). Scaffolding the academic language of complex text: An intervention for late secondary students. *Journal of Research in Reading, 44*(3), 508–528. http://doi.org/10.1111/1467–9817.12353

Rowling, J. K. (1998). *Harry Potter and the sorcerer's stone.* Scholastic.

Shanahan, T. (n.d.). Teaching with complex text. *Shanahan on Literacy.* https://www.shanahanonliteracy.com/publications/teaching-with-complex-text-1

Shanahan, T. (2021). Does text structure instruction improve reading comprehension? *Shanahan on Literacy.* https://www.shanahanonliteracy.com/blog/does-text-structure-instruction-improve-reading-comprehension#sthash.rsCwk7Hd.dpbs

Springer, S. E., Wilson, T. J., & Dole, J. A. (2014). Ready or not: Recognizing and preparing college ready students. *Journal of Adolescent & Adult Literacy, 58*(4), 299–307. http://doi.org/10.1002/jaal.363

Stereotypes and "single stories." (2018, March 12). Facing History & Ourselves. https://www.facinghistory.org/resource-library/teaching-holocaust-and-human-behavior/stereotypes-and-single-stories

Tolkien, J. R. R. (1954). *The lord of the rings.* Allen & Unwin.

Tovani, C. (2021). *Why do I have to read this?* Stenhouse.

University of Minnesota. (2022). Persuasive reasoning and fallacies. https://open.lib.umn.edu/communication/chapter/11-3-persuasive-reasoning-and-fallacies/#:~:text=Ten%20fallacies%20of%20reasoning%20discussed,herring%2C%20and%20appeal%20to%20tradition

Unrau, N. J., Rueda, R., Son, E., Polanin, J. R., Lundeen, R. J., & Muraszewski, A. K. (2018). Can reading self-efficacy be modified? A meta-analysis of the impact of interventions on reading self-efficacy. *Review of Educational Research, 88*(2), 167–204. http://doi.org/10.2102/0034654317743199

Vacca, R. T., Vacca, J. L., & Mraz, M. (2011). *Content area reading: Literacy and learning across the curriculum.* Pearson.

vanBergen, E., Vasalampi, K., & Torppa, M. (2020). How are practice and performance related? Development of reading from age 5 to 15. *Reading Research Quarterly, 56*(3), 415–434. http://doi.org/10.1002/rrq.309

Viorst, J. (1987). *Alexander and the terrible, horrible, no good, very bad day.* Atheneum.

Wexler, N. (2022, January 14). Not everyone needs college, but they do need to learn to read. *Forbes.* https://www.forbes.com/sites/nataliewexler/2022/01/14/not-everyone-needs-college-but-they-do-need-to-learn-to-read/?sh=64a1332b6281

YourDictionary. (2022). Archetype examples in literature. https://examples.yourdictionary.com/archetype-examples.html

Zusak, M. (2005). *The book thief.* Random House.

Chapter 8

Readers with Learning Disabilities and Learning Differences

Marian Moore-Taylor and Lin Carver

Mr. Elijah is one of the newest fifth-grade teachers at our school site; he was just hired last Friday! As the school year begins, he is nervous about teaching literacy skills because he assumed that since he was teaching fifth grade these students already knew how to read. As he was prepping for the first day of school, he realized that in addition to the fifth-grade science and math content, he was supposed to be helping his students (apparently many of them struggling readers) master reading. So, in distress, he went to hunt down the literacy coach.

"How am I supposed to instruct 22 students, who may or may not be on grade level, literacy skills? I thought I was just teaching content, after all they are in fifth grade and they should already know how to read, right?" he queried. "If they are in fifth grade and they can't read, then they have a reading disability and the ESE teacher should take care of that, right?"

"Well, some of them might have a reading disability, but some might just have a reading deficit," Serena, his literacy coach, responded.

"I don't get it. If they can't read after being in school for five years, what am I supposed to do? And what do you mean about the difference between reading deficits and disabilities? Aren't they the same thing?" Mr. Elijah asked.

"Not exactly," Serena replied. "A student may be struggling in reading, but that doesn't mean that they have a disability." Mr. Elijah was confused. How was he going to be able to distinguish between students who are having difficulty performing well in reading versus students who have actual reading disabilities? "When I agreed to teach fifth grade, I thought the students would be past all those issues!" he replied in confusion.

ANTICIPATION GUIDE

Read the following five statements before reading the chapter. Decide if you agree or disagree with each statement. Then read the chapter. After reading the chapter revisit the anticipation guide and decide if your views are the same or have changed.

1. Dyslexia is evidenced by word reversals.
2. Reading disabilities and reading difficulties are the same thing.
3. Decoding is the root of all reading difficulties.
4. Accommodations and modifications are synonymous.
5. Limited AT options are available.

SPEECH ACQUISITION VERSUS READING DEVELOPMENT

Unlike speech, which is an innate ability, reading is relatively new in its importance to the masses. The development of the printing press provided the general populace with access to large amounts of previously unavailable printed materials. Because of this invention, demand for books quickly expanded in the United States in the late 1700s and early 1800s. This was fueled by technological advances in paper manufacturing and reduced costs of materials to bind books (Creative Commons, 2013). The increased availability and amount of printed materials resulted in increasing the importance of proficient reading skills for the general populace.

For example, Poe (2011) reported over a decade ago that in the United States alone, about 3.1 billion books, 1,400 daily newspapers, and 19,000 magazines were published each year. The intervening time has resulted in an increase in that amount. Even technological advances have not decreased the need for proficient reading skills; use of reading skills is just expanding across several formats (Faverio & Perrin, 2022). Over 75% of U.S. adults indicate that they have read a book in the past year, comparable to the percentage in 2011 (Faverio & Perrin, 2022).

Many book publishers have embraced e-books as a way to adapt to new, changing technology through digital media and devices such as e-readers. In 2011, e-books became the number one format for adult fiction and young adult titles, surpassing printed materials (Sporkin, 2012) and shifting reading from print-based to digital presentation.

Consumers worldwide spend an average of 463 minutes or more than seven and a half hours per day engaged with media. Americans tend to average more time than most, as media is a major part of their daily lives. Even though exposure to media is changing, Americans still spend around 347 minutes per day (or more than five and a half hours) with print media, along with 470 minutes per day (or more than seven and a half hours) with digital media, thus reinforcing the paramount role reading plays even in the digital age (Statista Research Department, 2021).

High School versus College and Career Reading Levels

So as students prepare for life beyond their K–12 experience, the question is, at what level do they need to be able to read to be successful? Is just being able to read high school texts enough? There is a gap of 65L to 230L between materials used with high school seniors and those incorporated in postsecondary settings. The Lexile of materials used in many careers ranges from 1200L to 1400L, while typical high school textbooks for eleventh and twelfth graders range from 1050L to 1165L. This illustrates the importance of helping students read at a high school level or above. It is important to remember that a 250L difference between a reader's ability and the text complexity can result in a drop from 75% comprehension to 50% comprehension. This means that even high school seniors who can successfully read twelfth-grade texts may enter college or the workplace and encounter texts that result in less than 50% comprehension (Williamson, 2008). This is an even more significant problem for students who are struggling in reading because of disabilities or reading difficulties.

What Is a Learning Disability?

Learning disabilities are disorders that affect a person's ability to understand or use spoken or written language, complete mathematical calculations, coordinate movements, or direct attention appropriately. Although learning disabilities occur in very young children, the disorders are usually not recognized until the child reaches school age. About 8 to 10% of children in the United States under the age of 18 have some type of learning disability (NINDS, 2022). Learning disabilities can be the result of genetic or neurobiological factors that affect one or more of the cognitive processes. These processing problems can interfere with the acquisition of basic skills such as reading, writing, and math. However, they can also interfere with higher level skills such as organization, time management, abstract reasoning, long-term memory, short-term memory, and attention (Learning Disabilities Association of America, 2022).

Learning disabilities are not just related to academic achievement; they can impact relationships with family, friends, and colleagues at work or school.

Individuals with learning disabilities (LD) may experience difficulty learning particular skills or academic areas, but learning disabilities are not related to intelligence since generally people with learning disabilities are of average or above average intelligence. Frequently the learning disability is evidenced by a gap between individuals' potential and their actual academic achievement. A learning disability (LD) cannot be cured or fixed, but with support and intervention these individuals with learning disabilities can be successful in school and beyond (Learning Disabilities Association of America, 2022).

Learning disabilities are often physiological, in that the brain of someone with a learning disability may be wired differently than the brains of others (though not better or worse). However, we are concerned about learning disabilities here because it has been estimated that up to 80% of these disabilities present as problems learning to read (Drummond, n.d.). Most of the learning disabilities that are related to reading deficits stem from phonological processing issues. The part of the brain in which this processing occurs for LD students is wired differently, which can indicate a neuropsychological abnormality (Frank, 2014). Abnormalities in the brain could hinder the visual and auditory responses that affect students' abilities to discriminate among various sounds and letter symbols. As LD students are exposed to reading skills, the left perisylvian region of the brain is disrupted, causing the students to misinterpret written words (Frank, 2014). Additionally, neuropsychological abnormalities interfere with the brain's prefrontal lobes, the areas responsible for long- and short-term memory (Frank, 2014). The long- and short-term memory is paramount for learning new information.

Neuroscientist Sally Shaywitz's work on LDs expounded on the role of the left hemisphere and prefrontal brain lobes in word analysis, articulation, and word recognition. Shaywitz et al. (2008) examined how the brain functions during reading using a functional magnetic resonance imaging (fMRI) tool. This tool was used to compare the neuroimaging of the anterior network, the part of the brain responsible for language processing; the parieto-temporal lobe, the part of the brain responsible for spoken and written language; and the occipito-temporal lobe, the part of the brain responsible for visual perception of impaired and nonimpaired students. Shaywitz et al.'s study determined that LD students' left hemisphere brain activity functioned differently during reading (Shaywitz et al., 2008). In other words, while reading, students with neuropsychological abnormalities displayed differences in the left hemisphere of the brain, making it more difficult for them to process written language.

Learning disorders can vary in severity; they may be classified as mild, moderate, or severe (Soares & Patel, 2015). A mild intensity is evidenced by some difficulties with learning in one or two academic areas. A moderate level of disability is evidenced by significant difficulties with learning that require some specialized teaching and some accommodations or supportive services. A severe disability is one that is affecting several academic areas and requires ongoing intensive specialized teaching (American Psychiatric Association, 2022).

Specific Learning Disabilities

Specific learning disability (SLD) is characterized as a neurological-based learning abnormality that hinders children from reaching academic success (Frank, 2014). SLD can be defined as "a disorder in one or more of the basic psychological processes involved in understanding or in using language, spoken or written, that may manifest itself in the imperfect ability to listen, think, speak, read, write, spell or do mathematical calculations, including conditions such as perceptual disabilities, brain injury, minimal brain dysfunction, dyslexia, and developmental aphasia" (Fiedler, 2022, para. 1). SLD excludes deficits in visual, hearing, motor disabilities, intellectual disability, or serious emotional disability. It also does not include environmental or economic disadvantages or limited English proficiencies.

Instead, children who have SLD may possess intellectual stability, appear to have normal vision and hearing, and have no record of medical diseases but still perform poorly in several academic content areas (Frank, 2014). SLDs can also negatively affect students' motor skills and coordination as well as behavior and social contentment (Frank, 2014). However, SLD is usually evidenced by reading, writing, or math deficiencies. It is a broad term that encompasses seven different types of learning disabilities according to the Learning Disabilities Association of America: dyslexia, dysgraphia, dyscalculia, auditory processing disorder, language processing disorder, nonverbal learning disabilities, and visual perceptual deficit (Muktamath et al., 2021). These are explained in more detail in the following sections.

NON-READING-RELATED LEARNING DISABILITIES

Although LDs often impact reading development, not all learning disabilities impact reading.

Dyscalculia

Dyscalculia is a specific LD that affects an individual's ability to understand numbers and learn math facts; it is estimated that 5 to 10% of people might have dyscalculia (Understood Team, 2022). Dyscalculia may be apparent in a couple of, or many, transferable areas of mathematics. Generally, dyscalculia refers to an impairment in number sense, rote memorization of math facts, and accurate math calculation and reasoning (Soares & Patel, 2015). However, the term "dyscalculia" refers to obstacles with numerology and number sense, which is a neurological deficiency. This means that this disability only affects people who experience difficulties in the areas of mathematics that deal with numbers (Emerson & Babtie, 2015). Difficulties may be evidenced in grasping the meaning of quantities, understanding the relationship between the numeral and the word, remembering mathematical facts, counting money, estimating time, judging speed or distance, understanding mathematic logic, or holding numbers in short-term memory (Soares & Patel, 2015).

A child may exhibit the key factors of dyscalculia through a significant inability to instantly recognize the number of objects in a small group without counting them, or subitize (Emerson & Babtie, 2015). Several cognitive neurologists have concluded that newborns should have the ability to subitize. If not, these children may possess a deficit in their brains that causes them to process numerology at a much slower rate than their peers (Butterworth & Kovas, 2013). Of course, subitizing is not the only issue to be considered in determining a numerology disability. Other cognitive disabilities, such as language delay and dyslexia, can hinder children's ability to express and process mathematical concepts and vocabulary (Emerson & Babtie, 2015).

Dysgraphia

It is estimated, based upon a study in the journal *Translational Pediatrics*, that approximately 10 to 30% of children experience difficulty with writing (Borst, 2021). Dysgraphia is a specific LD that affects how individuals process visual-spatial information. These learners experience difficulty organizing letters, numbers, words, and lines of text (Gehsmann & Templeton, 2022). This difficulty becomes apparent in a person's handwriting ability and fine motor skills. Differences between students' oral expression and written composition may also be evident.

Dysgraphia can stem from fine motor control difficulties, visual-motor perception problems, and kinesthesia issues, which can result in slow or poorly formed letters and words. Students may demonstrate reduced writing fluency, deficient writing stamina, omitting words in written sentences, difficulty with written syntax and grammar, and inconsistent spacing and alignment of numbers or letters. A few fine motor skills that students with dysgraphia lack are simple tasks like tapping their fingers, gripping an object, determining the appropriate amount of force to use when gripping an object, and sustaining fine motor activities (Chung & Patel, 2015).

Stephen Glicksman, a developmental psychologist at Makor Disability Services and adjunct professor at Yeshiva University, supported the neurological base for this disability by indicating "people with dysgraphia are wired differently when it comes to writing" (Borst, 2021, para. 6).

Nonverbal Learning Disabilities

Nonverbal learning disability (NVLD), a comparatively new discovery, was first identified and described in 1967 (Margolis et al., 2020). This particular disability is often misdiagnosed or underdiagnosed; consequently the prevalence of the disorder is unclear. It appears that the condition affects boys and girls equally, and because it tends to run in families this suggests a genetic component (Psychology Today, 2022).

Students with nonverbal learning disabilities may have trouble interpreting nonverbal cues such as facial expressions or body language; may have poor coordination; and may experience difficulty managing visual-spatial information such as drawing, writing, or telling time. NVLD is characterized by deficits in social perceptions, social behaviors, and cognitive and motor difficulties; these activities occur in the right hemisphere of the brain (Cornoldi et al., 2016). In spite of a large vocabulary, strong memory, and good verbal skills, individuals may experience difficulty with reading comprehension and mathematical word problems that require spatial visualization or pattern recognition (Psychology Today, 2022).

Attention-Deficit/Hyperactivity Disorder (ADHD)

Attention-deficit/hyperactivity disorder (ADHD) is characterized by ongoing patterns of inattention and/or hyperactivity-impulsivity that interferes with functioning or development (National Institutes of Health, 2022). It is usually diagnosed in elementary school, and for this particular diagnosis, the symptoms must have been present before the age of 12 (National Institutes of Health, 2022). ADHD is more common in males than females, and females with ADHD are more likely to primarily have inattention symptoms. People with ADHD often have other conditions, such as SLDs, anxiety disorder, conduct disorder, depression, and substance abuse (National Institutes of Health, 2022).

This disorder includes difficulty staying focused and paying attention, controlling behavior, and hyperactivity. Inattention is often evidenced by overlooked or missed details, seeming not to listen when spoken to, difficulty in follow-through on instructions, organizational or sequencing difficulties, loss of materials, frequent distractedness, or forgetfulness in daily activities. Hyperactivity-impulsivity, on the other hand, is evidenced by moving around when seated, leaving the seat, moving constantly, talking excessively, interrupting, or difficulty waiting for one's turn. It is often viewed as a hereditary disability that is passed on from parent to child; however, how ADHD is passed down through generations is unknown (Wender & Tomb, 2016). Researchers are examining other possible environmental factors such as brain injuries, nutrition, and social environments that might play a role in this disorder as well (National Institutes of Health, 2022).

Because there is no specific psychological assessment for detecting ADHD, ADHD is generally identified from the child's and the parents' mental history, observations by educators, and additional observations by anyone who spends a large amount of time with the child (Wender & Tomb, 2016). Although stimulants, psychotherapy, education, and training are used to treat ADHD symptoms, as with other disabilities, there is no cure (National Institutes of Health, 2022).

Dyspraxia

Dyspraxia, also known as developmental coordination disorder (DCD), causes difficulty with movement and coordination (gross motor skills). It can also impact fine motor skills such as writing or grasping and manipulating small objects. The cause of dyspraxia is unknown, but being born prematurely seems to place an individual at a higher risk for developing this disorder. Dyspraxia is more common in males and often runs in families (NHS, 2020).

Children affected with this disability have trouble participating in and remembering physical activities because the motor cortex in their brains fails to operate properly (Brookes, 2007). Dyspraxia hinders children from planning and moving instinctively because their mental connections in this area are missing or disrupted (Brookes, 2007).

Executive Dysfunction

Executive dysfunction describes a range of cognitive, behavioral, and emotional difficulties. Individuals with executive dysfunction struggle with planning, problem-solving, organization, and time and space management. Children with executive functioning problems struggle to organize materials, regulate emotions, develop schedules, and stick with tasks. They misplace papers, reports, and other materials at home and at school. Behavior modification programs like token systems and daily report cards generally work well; however, children may get bored with these systems. Similarly, daily report cards, while initially helpful, may end up making these children feel bad about themselves when they do not succeed, thus creating a negative reinforcement loop. Cognitive behavioral therapy can be helpful because it offers immediate interventions (Rodden, 2022).

Executive functioning (EF) has not been clearly defined, but it conveys several meanings and can be thought of as a set of higher cognitive skills responsible for many everyday activities and abilities such as planning, organizing, cognitive flexibility, working memory, monitoring, and self-regulation (Memisevic & Sinanovic, 2014). Mahone et al. (2002) define EF as self-regulatory behaviors necessary for selecting and sustaining actions and guiding behaviors in the context of rules (Memisevic & Sinanovic, 2014).

READING DIFFICULTY VERSUS READING DISORDER: WHAT'S THE DIFFERENCE?

Many of these disabilities will impact children's reading performance and achievement. Some students struggle with reading, but not every student who struggles has a diagnosed reading disability. The struggling nondisabled learners may have developed at a different pace than their peers; have required more time to master certain ideas or concepts; have needed specialized reading instruction different from the approach used in the classroom; or have previously received poor reading instruction, experienced frequent moves, missed instruction because of absences, or just not been able to focus because of other social, emotional, or attentional issues. Whatever the case, these students need proficient teachers to provide them with the reading help they need to be successful readers.

On the other hand, some students are formally diagnosed with an LD. These students should be receiving special education under a federal law called the Individuals with Disabilities Education Act (IDEA). Reading disabilities likely occur in at least 20% of the population (Shaywitz et al., 2003); however, only about 4% of school-age students receive special education services for reading disabilities.

TYPES OF READING DISORDERS

Dyslexia

Dyslexia is a SLD that affects reading and related language-based processing skills. It is most commonly a result of difficulty in phonological processing (the ability to distinguish the individual sounds of spoken language), which affects the ability of an individual to speak, read, spell, and, often, learn a second language (Yale Center for Dyslexia & Creativity, 2022). Dyslexia affects 20% of the population and impacts 80 to 90% of all those with LDs. It is the most common of all neurocognitive disorders (Yale Center for Dyslexia & Creativity, 2022).

The severity of the disorder varies, but the condition often becomes apparent as a child begins the process of learning to read. The signs of dyslexia can be difficult to recognize before a child enters school, but some early clues may indicate a problem. These include difficulty learning nursery rhymes and problems remembering or naming letters, numbers, and colors. Once a child reaches school age, the child's teacher may be the first to notice a problem since these differences become more evident. Children may experience difficulty processing and understanding what is heard, difficulty sequencing, challenges in spelling, needing longer time to complete reading and writing tasks, and an inability to sound out unfamiliar words (Mayo Clinic, 2022).

Contrary to what is sometimes espoused, dyslexia is not seeing letters mixed up or backwards, or seeing words mixed up or jumbled. This is a characteristic of a stage of development; it is typical for learners in kindergarten and first grade to reverse some letters. If they do not outgrow this difficulty by the end of second or the middle of third grade, then this challenge may indicate a difficulty with directionality, which may make reading and writing more difficult (Kennedy, 2022).

Dyslexia results from individual differences in the parts of the brain that enable reading. It tends to run in families and appears to be linked to certain genes that affect how the brain processes reading and language (Mayo Clinic, 2022).

SUPPORTING STUDENTS WITH READING DIFFICULTIES AND DISABILITIES

By law, individuals with a reading disability are entitled to accommodations under the IDEA and the Americans with Disabilities Act (ADA). Accommodations are not meant to give these students an advantage over their peers, but instead they are an attempt to level the playing field. Students with disabilities often experience challenges that interfere with their ability to access and demonstrate learning. These barriers can occur in the way the information is presented, the way the student is required to respond, the way the classroom is structured, or the timing or schedule of instruction (Iris Center, 2022).

Accommodations

Accommodations do not change the expectations for learning, reduce the requirement of the task, or change what the students are required to learn.

Providing extra time is one of the most frequently used accommodations. However, just providing extra time is not always the answer.

Instructional accommodations make changes in the way the information is delivered in the classroom. Following are examples of accommodations that might help students with three different disabilities. A child with a visual disability might profit from an audio version, large print materials, or Braille materials. A child with an SLD that is interfering with decoding the text might need audio books or text-to-speech programs. A child with ADHD might profit from frequent breaks or working directly in the text rather than transcribing onto a different paper (Iris Center, 2022). Allowing additional time to complete schoolwork and take tests can have a huge impact on a student's ability to demonstrate knowledge and succeed in school. Another helpful accommodation as students get older is to request a lighter course load so that they can avoid taking too many courses at the same time with large volumes of reading (Yale Center for Dyslexia & Creativity, 2022).

Modifications

Modifications, instructional strategies, and interventions are instructional practices that are often confused with accommodations. Instructional practices can be used to help improve students' learning. Modifications change the playing field by changing what students learn and providing more support than accommodations can provide. Modifications could also be provided for children with the three disabilities discussed previously. The child with the visual disability might have an alternate assignment if unable to read the printed text. The child with the SLD who is experiencing difficulty decoding the text could read a lower-level book. The child with ADHD might be asked to answer fewer homework questions (Iris Center, 2022). Accommodations or modifications can be high tech, low tech, or no tech.

Comprehension Difficulties

Students with LDs often struggle with higher-level thinking skills. Since students who are learning disabled require extensive modeling and practicing before their learning is associative, they have to use tremendous effort in actively thinking about learning. In addition, it is difficult for students with LDs to be involved in multiple processes simultaneously. "A major reason for the poor performance of many children with learning disabilities is failure to read strategically and spontaneously monitor understanding of what is being read" (Gersten et al., 2001, p. 291).

Specific genres of reading can be challenging for students with an SLD, especially expository text. Students with SLDs struggle with reading and comprehending expository text structures (DiCecco & Gleason, 2002; Gersten et al., 2001). These students also tend to develop understanding of text structure at a slower rate than their peers (Gersten et al., 2001).

It has been established that students who are learning disabled often need support in the area of reading comprehension. Five strategies have been proven to improve reading comprehension with these special needs students: explicit instruction, prior knowledge, theme identification, graphic organizers, and literature circles (Spencer, 2012). Although these strategies are effective with students who have LDs, they can also be used successfully with the general education population.

Basic Processing Weaknesses

Just teaching more comprehension strategies is not necessarily the answer. What may appear to be a reading comprehension problem may be caused by weaknesses in the basic skills required for the reading process. Students need to be able to accomplish each of these skills: quickly processing the printed text (reading speed), keeping track of what words are in the sentences (working memory), understanding vocabulary meaning and text conventions (semantics and grammar), and processing what is read (receptive language) (Cutting et al., 2009).

Long-Term Memory Difficulties

Difficulties with long-term visual memory can result in poor sight word recognition. A limited sight word vocabulary reduces reading speed, and available working memory is consumed by attempting to decode the words impacting comprehension (Elliott et al., 2010). During beginning instruction, children are exposed to a limited number of words that can be easily memorized. However, vocabulary expands dramatically through elementary school to approximately 2,000 to 3,000 new words each year (Biemeller, 2003); consequently, depending on visual memory becomes less effective. Students cannot memorize enough words over time, and so these students using only visual memory find that their word reading and reading comprehension decline with age (Shaywitz, 2005).

Short-Term or Working Memory Difficulties

Working memory capacity is often related to reading comprehension since working memory impacts the duration of time that a fact is retained and the probability that it will be consolidated into long-term memory. Students with more efficient working memory will have additional capacity and processing time for practicing and consolidating information, while poorer readers might require all their processing ability to perform a given task. As reading material becomes more difficult, readers may also experience difficulty comprehending texts they are reading, become tired during longer readings, and have increased frustration. Melby-Lervag et al. (2016) concluded that "there is no evidence that working memory training yields improvements in so-called far-transfer abilities. . . . Repetitively practicing simple memory tasks on a computer are unlikely to lead to generalized cognitive abilities" (p. 526). Difficulties with word reading and problems with reading and language comprehension can be improved by using a structured literacy approach to teaching oral language, reading, spelling, and writing skills. During intervention, it is important to focus on both repeated drill and practice to increase automaticity as well as various language opportunities within meaningful contexts.

Phonological Processing Difficulties

Early explicit instruction in phonemic awareness is the only strategy for children who are experiencing difficulty in this area. Phonemic awareness should first be taught without any letters, using blocks or chips to represent the sounds so that children learn to hear those sounds without being confused by the letters, since many times the same sound is represented by different letter combinations. They need to practice taking words apart auditorily and then putting them back together again.

Difficulties in the Sound-Symbol Relationship

After children learn to isolate and manipulate phonemes, single letters and letter combinations or families (e.g., "-at," "-up," "-in," etc.) are introduced. Rhyming and alliteration games can be used to reinforce these skills. Instruction in the sound-symbol relationships needs to be systematic and sequential, and to incorporate multiple modalities. The sequence for instruction in phonic elements needs to be specifically identified.

DIGITAL RESOURCES

While additional skills are being developed, assistive technology (AT) may support individuals with many different types of disabilities. These might include anything from cognitive problems to physical impairments. The use of AT can increase a child's self-reliance and sense of independence. Learners who struggle in school are often overly dependent on parents, siblings, friends, and teachers for help with assignments. By using AT, students can experience success while working independently (Stanberry & Raskind, 2009).

Note-Taking

The Livescribe Smartpen can simplify the process of in-class note-taking by capturing everything the student hears and writes. In addition, the user can transfer notes and recordings to a computer, so that notes can be easily searched and organized for studying. The audio recording can be slowed down or sped up as needed, and a specific section of any recording can be played back simply by tapping that part of the written notes (LiveScribe, 2022).

Speech-to-Text

The user "dictates" into a microphone, and their spoken words appear on the computer screen as text. This can help a user whose oral language ability is better than their writing skills. Dragon NaturallySpeaking is one example of a speech-to-text program that can provide support in a number of ways, including orally committing ideas to paper, dictating answers to homework, and writing essays. Other such programs include Google Cloud and Windows Speech Recognition (Collins, 2022).

Text-to-Speech

These systems can display and read aloud text on a computer screen, including text that has been typed by the user, has been scanned in from printed pages (e.g., books, letters), or appears on the internet. Read & Write Gold is an AT software program developed to improve learning. In addition to offering reading aloud of digitized text, other features include picture dictionaries, a thesaurus, and word prediction. Other examples of text-to-speech programs are Natural Reader and Read Aloud in Word. Digitized libraries such as Bookshare and Learning Ally also offer their own text-to-speech software (Stanberry & Raskind, 2009).

Abbreviation Expanders

For students who have difficulties with fine motor skills, abbreviation expanders can help to save keystrokes and reduce spelling concerns. These programs are used with word processing programs and allow students to create, store, and reuse abbreviations for frequently used words or phrases (Stanberry & Raskind, 2009).

Alternative Keyboards

Alternative keyboards are programmable and have special overlays that customize the appearance and function of a standard keyboard. Students who have LDs or have trouble typing may benefit from customization that reduces input choices, groups keys by color/location, and adds graphics to aid comprehension (Richards, n.d.).

Audiobooks and Publications

Recorded books allow users to listen to text and are available in a variety of formats. Special playback units allow users to search and bookmark pages and chapters. Subscription services offer extensive electronic library collections (Stanberry & Raskind, 2009).

Electronic Math Worksheets

Electronic math worksheets are software programs that can help students who have difficulty organizing, aligning, and working through problems on a computer screen. Onscreen numbers can also be read aloud. This may be helpful to people who have trouble aligning math problems with pencil and paper (Stanberry & Raskind, 2009).

Graphic Organizers and Outlining

Graphic organizers and outlining programs help learners who have difficulty organizing and outlining information as they prepare to work on a writing project. This type of program lets a user "dump" information in an unstructured manner and later helps organize the information into appropriate categories and order (Stanberry & Raskind, 2009).

Optical Character Recognition

This technology allows a student to scan printed material into a computer. The scanned text is then read aloud using a speech synthesis/screen reading system. Optical character recognition (OCR) is available as stand-alone units, computer software, and portable, pocket-sized devices (Stanberry & Raskind, 2009).

Personal FM Listening Systems

A personal FM listening system transmits a speaker's voice directly to the student's ear. This device may help the listener focus on what the speaker is saying. The unit consists of a wireless transmitter with a microphone that is worn by the speaker and a receiver with an earphone worn by the listener (Richards, n.d.).

Proofreading Programs

Students who struggle with spelling, grammar, punctuation, word usage, and sentence structure may benefit from software programs included in many word processing systems that scan word processing documents and alert the user to possible errors. Grammarly and Chrome extensions are programs that can be used to support learners (Max, 2022).

Talking Calculators

A talking calculator has a built-in speech synthesizer that reads aloud each number, symbol, or operation key a user presses; it also vocalizes the answer to the problem. This auditory feedback may help the learner check the accuracy of the keys pressed and verify the answer before it is transferred to paper (Richards, n.d.).

Talking Spell Checkers and Electronic Dictionaries

Talking spell checkers and electronic dictionaries can help a student experiencing difficulty in spelling to select or identify appropriate words and to correct spelling errors during the writing and proofreading stages. Talking devices "read aloud" and display the selected words onscreen, so the student can see and hear the words.

Word Prediction Programs

Word prediction software can help a student during word processing by "predicting" a word the learner intends to type. Predictions are based on spelling, syntax, and frequent/recent use. This program helps students who struggle with writing to use proper spelling, grammar, and word choices, with fewer keystrokes.

ANTICIPATION GUIDE REVISITED

At the beginning of the chapter, you examined five statements. Based upon what you have read in this chapter, revisit the anticipation guide statements and decide if your views are the same or have changed.

1. Dyslexia is evidenced by word reversals.
2. Reading disabilities and reading difficulties are the same thing.
3. Decoding is the root of all reading difficulties.
4. Accommodations and modifications are synonymous.
5. Limited AT options are available.

CONCLUSION

Students may struggle with reading for a variety of reasons. They may have an SLD, or they may just have reading difficulties. Each of the LDs has its own characteristics and frequency. However, many of these disabilities will impact reading development.

Many different foundational skills work together to result in comprehension; consequently, it is important to identify the specific area where children are experiencing difficulty. The specific foundational skills where difficulties are occurring need to be addressed so that growth may occur. Just providing additional instruction in comprehension strategies is not necessarily the answer. While teachers are working with students to address areas where they are experiencing difficulty, AT might provide much-needed support to allow these students to be more successful.

STOP AND THINK

1. Compare the frequency and characteristics of two students with different disabilities that you have, have had, or may have in your classroom. Identify a piece of adaptive technology that would be helpful for each learner.
2. Identify two students with disabilities in your classroom. Identify one accommodation and one modification that might be appropriate for each student. Explain why these would be appropriate for each student.

REFERENCES

American Psychiatric Association. (2022). What is specific learning disorder? https://psychiatry.org/patients-families/specific-learning-disorder/what-is-specific-learning-disorder

Biemiller, A. (2003). Vocabulary: Needed if more children are to read well. *Reading Psychology*, 24(3–4), 323–335.

Borst, H. (2021, December 13). What is dysgraphia? *US News and World Report*. https://www.usnews.com/education/k12/articles/what-is-dysgraphia#:~:text=Although%20the%20exact%20prevalence%20of,in%20the%20journal%20Translational%20Pediatrics.

Brookes, G. (2007). *Dyspraxia* (2nd ed.). Continuum International Publishing Group.

Chung, P., & Patel, D. R. (2015). Dysgraphia. *International Journal of Child and Adolescent Health*, 8(1), 27–36. https://saintleo.idm.oclc.org/login?url=https://www-proquest-com.saintleo.idm.oclc.org/scholarly-journals/dysgraphia/docview/1705545841/se-2

Collins, B. (2022). Best speech to text software for 2022: 8 top choices. Become a Writer Today. https://becomeawritertoday.com/speech-to-text/

Cornoldi, C., Mammarella, I. C., & Goldenring Fine, J. (2016). *Nonverbal learning disabilities*. Guilford Press.

Creative Commons. (2013). *Communication in the real world: An introduction to communication studies*. University of Minnesota Libraries. https://open.lib.umn.edu/communication/front-matter/publisher-information/

Cutting, L. E., Materek, A., Cole, C. A., Levine, T. M., & Mahone, E. M. (2009). Effects of fluency, oral language, and executive function on reading comprehension performance. *Annals of Dyslexia*, 59(1), 34–54.

DiCecco, V. M., & Gleason, M. M. (2002). Using graphic organizers to attain relational knowledge from expository text. *Journal of Learning Disabilities*, 35(4), 306–320.

Drummond, K. (n.d.). About reading disabilities, learning disorders, and reading difficulties. Reading Rockets. https://www.readingrockets.org/article/about-reading-disabilities-learning-disabilities-and-reading-difficulties

Elliott, C. D., Hale, J. B., Fiorello, C. A., Dorvil, C., & Moldovan, J. (2010). Differential ability scales–II prediction of reading performance: Global scores are not enough. *Psychology in the Schools*, 47(7), 698–720.

Emerson, J., & Babtie, P. (2015). *Understanding dyscalculia and numeracy difficulties: A guide for parents, teachers and other professionals*. Jessica Kingsley Publishers.

Faverio, M., & Perrin, A. (2022, January 6). Three-in-ten Americans now read e-books. Pew Research Center. https://www.pewresearch.org/fact-tank/2022/01/06/three-in-ten-americans-now-read-e-books/

Fiedler, V. (2022, July 7). Specific learning disability (SLD). CDE. https://www.cde.state.co.us/cdesped/sd-sld

Frank, Y. (2014). *Specific learning disabilities*. Oxford University Press.

Gehsmann, K. M., & Templeton, S. (2022). *Teaching reading and writing: The developmental approach* (2nd ed.). Pearson.

Gersten, R., Fuchs, L. S., Williams, J. P., & Baker, S. (2001). Teaching reading comprehension strategies to students with learning disabilities: A review of research. *Review of Educational Research, 71*(2), 279–320.

Iris Center. (2022). Understanding accommodations. https://iris.peabody.vanderbilt.edu/micro-credential/micro-accommodations/p01/

Kennedy, D. (2022). What dyslexia isn't. Mindspark: Custom Learning Solutions. https://mindsparklearning.com/what-dyslexia-isnt/

Learning Disabilities Association of America. (2022). Types of learning disabilities. https://ldaamerica.org/types-of-learning-disabilities/

LiveScribe. (2022). Pioneering smart pens. https://us.livescribe.com/

Mahone, E. M., Hagelthorn, K. M., Cutting, L. E., Schuerholz, L. J., Felletier, S., Rawlins, C., Singer, H. S., & Denckla, M. B. (2002). Effects of IQ on executive function measures in children with ADHD. *Child Neuropsychology, 8*(1), 52–65. https://pubmed.ncbi.nlm.nih.gov/12610776/

Margolis, A. E., Broitman, J., & Davis, J. M. (2020). Learning disability among North American children and adolescents. *JAMA Network Open, 3*(4). https://doi.10.1001/jamanetworkopen.2020.2551

Max, T. (2022). The best free and paid proofreading and editing software to use in 2022. Scribe Media. https://scribemedia.com/proofreading-editing-software/

Mayo Clinic. (2022). Dyslexia. https://www.mayoclinic.org/diseases-conditions/dyslexia/symptoms-causes/syc-20353552#:~:text=Dyslexia%20is%20a%20learning%20disorder,the%20brain%20that%20process%20language.

Melby-Lervag, M., Redick, T. S., & Hulme, C. (2016, July 29). Working memory training does not improve performance on measures of intelligence of other measures of "far transfer": Evidence from a meta-analytic review. *Perspectives on Psychological Science, 11*(4), 512–534. https://journals.sagepub.com/doi/full/10.1177/1745691616635612

Memisevic, H., & Sinonovic, O. (2014). Executive function in children with intellectual disability—The effects of sex, level and aetiology of intellectual disability. *Journal of Intellectual Disability Research, 58*(9), 830–837. https://psycnet.apa.org/doi/10.1111/jir.12098"https://doi.org/10.1111/jir.12098

Muktamath, V. U., Hegde, P. R., & Chand, S. (2021, December 10). Types of learning disability. In Sandro Misciagna (Ed.), *Learning disabilities: Neurobiology, assessment, clinical features and treatments.* https://www.intechopen.com/chapters/79619

National Institute of Neurological Disorder and Stroke (NINDS). (2022). Learning disabilities. https://www.ninds.nih.gov/health-information/disorders/learning-disabilities?search-term=types%20of%20learning%20disabilities

National Institutes of Health. (2022). Attention-deficit/hyperactivity disorder. https://www.nimh.nih.gov/health/topics/attention-deficit-hyperactivity-disorder-adhd#:~:text=Attention%2Ddeficit%2Fhyperactivity%20disorder%20(,interferes%20with%20functioning%20or%20development

NHS. (2020, October 1). Dyspraxia (developmental co-ordination disorder) in adults. https://www.nhs.uk/conditions/developmental-coordination-disorder-dyspraxia-in-adults/#:~:text=Dyspraxia%2C%20also%20known%20as%20developmental,learning%20to%20drive%20a%20car

Poe, M. T. (2011). *A history of communications: Media and society from the evolution of speech to the internet.* Cambridge.

Psychology Today. (2022). Nonverbal learning disorder. https://www.psychologytoday.com/us/conditions/nonverbal-learning-disorder

Richards, L. (n.d.). Assistive technology for students with learning disabilities from Mapcon.com. https://www.mapcon.com/us-en/assistive-technology-for-students-with-learning-disabilities-from-mapcon

Rodden, J. (2022, July 11). What is executive dysfunction? Signs and symptoms of EFD. *ADDitude.* https://www.additudemag.com/what-is-executive-function-disorder/#:~:text=Executive%20dysfunction%20is%20a%20term,%2C%20organization%2C%20and%20time%20management

Shaywitz, S. (2005). *Overcoming dyslexia: A new and complete science-based program for reading problems at any level.* Vintage.

Shaywitz, S. E., Morris, R., & Shaywitz, B. A. (2008). The education of dyslexic children from childhood to young adulthood. *Annual Review of Psychology, 59*(1), 451–475. https://doi.org/10.1146/annurev.psych.59.103006.093633

Shaywitz, S. E., Shaywitz, B. A., Fulbright, R. K., Skudlarski, W. Nencl, W. E., Constable, R. T., Pugh, K. R., Holahan, J. M., Marchione, K. E., Fletcher, J. M., Lyon, G. R., & Gore, J. C. (2003). Neural systems for compensation and persistence: Young adult outcome of childhood reading disability. *Biological Psychiatry, 1*(54), 25–33. doi:10.1016/s0006-3223(02)01836-x

Soares, N., & Patel, D. R. (2015). Dyscalculia. *International Journal of Child and Adolescent Health, 8*(1), 15–26. https://saintleo.idm.oclc.org/login?url=https://www-proquest-com.saintleo.idm.oclc.org/scholarly-journals/dyscalculia/docview/1705546083/se-2

Spencer, K. (2012). Reading comprehension: Five strategies for elementary students with learning disabilities. *Michigan Reading Journal, 45*(1), 15–22.

Sporkin, A. (2012, July 23). Bookstats 2012 highlights: Annual survey captures size and scope of US publishing industry. https://www.frontgatemedia.com/1066/

Stanberry, K., & Raskind, M. H. (2009). Assistive technology for kids with learning disabilities: An overview. Reading Rockets. https://www.readingrockets.org/article/assistive-technology-kids-learning-disabilities-overview

Statista Research Department, (2021, November 2). Media use in the U.S.: Statistics and facts. https://www.statista.com/topics/1536/media-use/#dossierKeyfigures

Understood Team. (2022). What is dyscalculia? https://www.understood.org/en/articles/what-is-dyscalculia?_sp=7098d37a-cf09–4647-aa8c-9985f21f76b0.1661457951532#Possible_causes_of_dyscalculia

Wender, P. H., & Tomb, D. A. (2016). *ADHD: Attention-deficit hyperactivity disorder in children, adolescents, and adults* (5th ed.). Oxford University Press. http://public.ebookcentral.proquest.com/choice/publicfullrecord.aspx?p=4706419.

Williamson, G. L. (2008). A text readability continuum for postsecondary readiness. *Journal of Advanced Academics, 19* (4), 602–632.
Yale Center for Dyslexia & Creativity. (2022). Dyslexia FAQ. https://dyslexia.yale.edu/dyslexia/dyslexia-faq/#:~:text=How%20common%20is%20dyslexia%3F,of%20all%20neuro%2Dcognitive%20disorders.

Index

abbreviation expanders, 165
ABC books, 31–32, 35
ABC graphic organizer, 119
academic language, 45, 55, 84, 104–105, 117, 132
academic vocabulary, 8, 45, 81, 83, 104
accommodations, 152, 154, 160–61, 167
active/passive voice, 136–37
active view of reading, 4–5, 12
advertisements, 94
affix, 66, 81, 84
alliteration, 20, 29, 82, 107, 134, 163
alphabetic principle, 10, 28, 42
alternative keyboards, 165
annotation, 119, 143–44
archetypes, 128, 134–35, 147
assistive technology, 164
attention, 5–6, 11, 21, 69, 103, 119, 136, 153, 157, 159
attention-deficit/hyperactivity disorder (ADHD), 157–58, 161
auditory discrimination, 21
automaticity, 7, 23–24, 45, 52, 71, 163

background knowledge, 2, 7, 24, 27, 46, 50, 55, 65, 79, 88, 91, 110–11, 116–17, 128, 131, 137
backwards outlining, 145
balanced literacy, 2, 4, 12, 54

base word, 66, 84, 133
before-, during-, after- reading, 50, 56–57, 65, 68, 73, 82, 89, 91, 92, 107–108, 112, 115, 120, 145
big books, 24, 26, 47
biography, 111, 112
blog, 91, 112, 142, 143
buddy reading, 71, 85

character resume, 139–40
choral reading, 28, 54
claim-evidence-reasoning, 82
class book, 32, 54
close reading, 108, 118
cognitive processes, 5, 153
coherence, 8–9
cohesion, 8–9
collaboration, 74, 85, 95, 109, 121
collaborative writing, 32
comics, 92
comic strip creator, 93, 120
compare/contrast graphic organizer, 68, 76, 142
complex text, 49, 66, 80, 85, 95, 104, 118, 129, 131–34, 137–38, 141, 143
comprehension, 5–7, 19, 24, 27, 30, 44–47, 50, 52, 54–56, 65–66, 71, 73, 81, 83, 85, 87–89, 91, 95, 100, 104, 107–108, 110–11, 116, 119–21,

132–33, 137–38, 146, 153, 157, 161–63, 165, 167
concept cubes, 116
concept map, 140–41
concept of word, 10, 19, 29, 42–43, 57
concrete operational, 80, 102
connected text, 4, 46, 49, 52
critical thinking, 7–9, 19, 27, 49, 73, 74, 88, 91, 117, 127, 141
cueing systems, 46–47, 54

decodable text, 6, 42, 52, 54, 57
decoding, 4–7, 10–11, 18–19, 22–23, 26, 44, 46, 51, 52, 65, 81, 104–105, 109, 111, 119, 152, 161, 167
derivational suffix, 80, 81, 95
describing characters, 31
digital literacy, 3, 109
digital media, 152, 153
digraph, 64, 76
diphthong, 64, 76
directionality, 10, 23, 32, 46, 160
discourse, 6–9, 45
Dolch list, 44, 65
double-entry journals, 138–39
drama, 111
dump and clump, 114
dyscalculia, 155–56
dysgraphia, 155–57
dyslexia, 152, 155, 156, 159–61, 167
dyspraxia, 158
dystopia, 115, 116

echo reading, 1, 29, 53
Elkonin boxes, 50
encoding, 6, 7, 9–11, 26
engagement, 2, 12, 46, 51, 65, 87, 111, 113, 120–21, 141
environmental print, 23–24, 26
executive dysfunction, 158
executive function, 6, 7, 9, 137, 158–59

fairy tales, 67–68, 76
fantasy, 21, 70–71, 92
field notes, 72

figurative language, 66, 82, 129, 131, 134
fill-in-the-blank message, 50–51
fishbowl discussion, 110, 112–13
Flipgrid, 56
fluency, 6, 10, 24, 26, 53, 65–66, 71, 83, 104, 110–11, 121, 137, 156
folktale, 1, 89

genre, xx, 9, 35, 45, 47–49, 57, 67, 70–71, 72, 74–76, 82, 85–86, 88–90, 92, 113, 115, 138, 162
gradual release, 49, 56, 121, 138
grammar, 18, 87, 88, 100, 110, 121, 156, 162, 166, 167
grand conversation, 1
grapheme, 20, 44
graphic novels, 74, 91, 119–20
graphic organizer, 68, 76, 86–87, 89, 91, 92–93, 107, 115, 119, 133, 140–41, 162, 165
guided practice, 25, 49, 107, 138
guided reading, 1, 5, 26, 64

handwriting, 6, 26, 67, 156
high-frequency, 25, 26, 42–46, 48, 57
hyperbole, 82, 89, 134

idiom, 8, 82, 134
independent reading, 5, 26, 54, 66, 112, 120
inference, 9, 46, 65, 74, 92–93, 110, 138, 144
inflectional suffixes, 45, 64, 67, 76, 81
informational text, 11, 54–55, 57, 66, 79, 81–83, 86, 104, 107, 117, 129, 132, 136, 142–43
interactive writing, 51
It Says-I Say-and So, 92–93

journal, 2, 48, 56, 73, 76, 112, 138–39, 142, 156; first-person journals, 73, 76
juicy sentences, 110

know-want to know-learn (KWL), 55, 107–108

learning disability (LD), 151, 153–155, 157, 161
letter identification, 24
letter-sound, 5, 23, 26, 44, 52, 105
leveled text, 26, 42, 49, 52–54, 57
loaded words, 94

mentor text, 1, 75, 86, 88
metaphor, 66, 82, 85, 90, 110, 134
modeling, 8, 25, 49, 69, 86, 93, 107, 112, 137, 143, 161
modifications, 152, 161, 167
morning message, 41–43, 46, 49–51, 57
morphemes, 11, 45, 84
motivation, 5, 11, 46, 51, 66, 69, 73, 83, 85, 95, 111, 113, 119, 121
mystery, 72
myths, 90

narrative pyramid, 114
nonverbal learning disability, 155, 157
note-taking, 85, 91, 164
nursery rhymes, 21, 26, 29, 30, 35, 160

onset, 20, 22–23, 26
optical character recognition, 166
oral language, 18–19, 22–23, 28, 34–35, 45, 48, 54, 163, 164
orthographic, 5–6, 52
orthographic mapping, 5–6

Padlet, 120
personal FM listening system, 166
personal word lists, 115–116
personification, 82, 134
phonemes, 19–20, 22, 26, 43, 44, 163
phonemic awareness, 5, 10, 18–22, 24, 29, 34, 44–45, 48–49, 52, 163
phonics, 5, 6, 12, 24, 26, 42, 44, 47–49, 51, 52–53, 57, 63, 64, 75, 83, 100, 104–105, 110, 121

phonological awareness, 4–5, 6–7, 10, 18, 20, 25–26, 29, 34, 104
phonological processing difficulties, 163
picture books, 26, 30, 33, 35, 45, 47, 49, 130
picture walk, 17, 27, 52
point around the picture, 28
point of view, 34, 70, 80, 104
predictable pattern, 24, 26, 28, 35, 53
prediction, 27, 33, 56, 65, 87, 89, 108, 114, 116, 164, 167
prediction relay, 89
prefix, 8, 84, 107, 132–33
prefrontal cortex, 102–103, 137
primary and secondary sources, 81
print concepts, 18, 23, 25–26, 32, 34
probable passage, 87–88
proofreading programs, 166
punctuation, 11, 23, 46, 48, 51, 99, 166

questioning, 8, 82, 145, 146
questioning the author (QtA), 145–147

read aloud, 11, 17, 24–27, 31, 45, 47, 56, 66, 73, 74–75, 86, 89, 164, 165, 166
reading buddies, 55, 71
reading rate, 11, 64, 80, 103, 156, 162
register, 8–9
repeated readings, 52, 71
rhetoric, 131, 135
rhyme time, 30
rhyming, 18, 20–22, 25–26, 29–30, 32, 34–35, 48, 68, 160, 163
rime, 20–23, 26
role, audience, format, and topic (RAFT), 141, 142
root word, 8, 81, 84, 107

Scarborough's reading rope, 5, 7
scavenger hunt, 79, 143
Science of Reading, 5, 44, 52, 54, 73
self-efficacy, 131, 148
self-help, 73–74, 75
self-monitoring, 47, 51, 138

semantic feature map, 120
shared reading, 5, 24–26, 47
share the pen, 31
short vowel, 48, 52, 53, 64–65, 105
sight words, 6, 11, 42–44, 46, 48, 57, 64–66, 71, 72, 76, 162
Simple View of Reading, 4–6, 12, 44
sketch to stretch, 55
social emotional learning, 56, 70, 73–74
social media, 56, 94
somebody wanted but so (SWBS), 69
sound-symbol, 4, 5, 52, 104, 163
specific learning disabilities (SLD), 155, 161–62
speeches, 140
speech-to-text, 164
spelling, 4, 10, 19, 23–24, 44, 48, 51, 64, 67, 86, 160, 163, 165–167
stamina, 66, 156
stop and jot, 56
story map, 68
stereotypes, 134, 140
structural analysis, 84, 105, 107, 132–33
structured literacy, 2, 4, 12, 163
suffix, 8, 45, 64, 67, 76, 80–81, 84, 95, 107, 133
summarize, 11, 65, 70, 82, 89, 116, 119
syllables, 20–22, 26, 46, 48, 64–65, 81, 105–106, 129
syntax, 4, 6, 50, 83, 110, 132, 136, 156, 167

t chart, 34, 89
talking calculators, 166
talking spell checkers, 166
tall tales, 89–90

text feature, 63, 66, 72, 79, 83
text reformulation, 88, 95
text structure, 81, 130, 132, 142–43, 162
text talk, 73
text-to-speech, 161
think aloud, 56, 119, 142
think-pair-share, 74, 75
3-2-1, 116
tone, 8, 9, 136
turn and talk, 85, 127, 141
Twister Spell and Read, 53

Venn diagram, 55, 113
vocabulary, 7–8, 10–11, 18–19, 24–25, 27, 29, 32, 42–43, 45–47, 50, 53, 65, 71, 73, 76, 80–84, 87–88, 91, 95, 104–107, 109–111, 115, 116–20, 121, 129, 132–33, 137, 143, 156–57, 162
vocabulary knowledge scales, 117, 118
vowel team, 64, 105

whole language, 4, 12
word cloud, 117
word ladders, 50–51
wordless books, 26–27, 35
word prediction programs, 167
word recognition, 4, 5, 6, 7, 26, 43, 111, 154, 162
word study, 4, 84
word wall, 26, 32
working memory, 6, 102, 159, 162–63
writing conventions, 67, 86, 136
writing process, 4, 9, 32, 48, 63, 66, 75, 86, 111

About the Editor and Contributors

Lin Carver, PhD

Lin Carver joined Saint Leo University after more than 30 years of experience in pre-K–12 education as a teacher, coach, and director in various settings. She currently serves as the director of program approval in the College of Education and Social Services and as program administrator for the master's in reading program. She is a professor in graduate education, where she teaches and chairs dissertations in the graduate studies in education programs (reading, instructional leadership, and educational leadership doctorate). Her passions include literacy, technology, and professional development.

Lisa Ciganek, EdD

Lisa Ciganek is an associate professor in the College of Educator Preparation and Leadership at Southeastern University. She teaches undergraduate courses; coordinates the master's in literacy education; and serves as the university's liaison to Crystal Lake Elementary, a community partnership school. Using over 20 years' experience as a teacher, coach, and professional developer, Lisa invests her time in producing high-quality teachers who are prepared for today's classrooms. Her research interests include literacy, teacher preparation, and trauma-informed education.

Janet Deck, EdD

Janet Deck is a professor of education at Southeastern University in Lakeland, Florida. Her passion is teaching literacy to education students. She writes literacy curriculum for the university and has led several programs, including the MEd in literacy education. Janet lives in the Blue Ridge

Mountains of North Georgia and enjoys hiking and pickleball. She has four awesome adult children and six even more awesome grandchildren.

Cheri Gallman, EdD

Cheri Gallman teaches as an adjunct professor at Saint Leo University in the Graduate Education Program. She also teachers middle school language arts for an online virtual school and serves on its research committee. As an educator and online learning specialist, she is passionate about helping students and teachers thrive both online and in traditional classrooms. Cheri is an avid animal lover and lives on a small farm with dogs, cats, horses, cows, goats, and emus and enjoys sharing her passion for animals with her family and friends.

Marian Moore-Taylor, EdD

Marian Moore-Taylor is an adjunct professor, instructor, and dissertation chair who currently works with elementary school teachers, administrators, and other educators by providing services that support educational advancement at Saint Leo University and Western Governors University. With 16 years of experience, she believes that educators should understand and implement effective classroom strategies so that every child has an opportunity to reach their educational goals. She lives in Florida with her husband and two children.

Gretchen Rudolph-Fladd, EdD

Gretchen Rudolph-Fladd is an elementary school principal at Pasco County Schools in central Florida. She has been a public educator for over 24 years. She is a graduate of Saint Leo University, where she received her EdD in school leadership, her MA in educational leadership, and her BA in elementary education. Her passion is early literacy, and she believes that a strong foundation in elementary school sets up all students for success.

www.ingramcontent.com/pod-product-compliance
Lightning Source LLC
Chambersburg PA
CBHW032046300426
44117CB00009B/1206